Reason and Commitment

Reason and Commitment

ROGER TRIGG

Senior Lecturer in Philosophy, University of Warwick

CAMBRIDGE UNIVERSITY PRESS

CAMBRIDGE

LONDON · NEW YORK · MELBOURNE

Published by the Syndics of the Cambridge University Press
The Pitt Building, Trumpington Street, Cambridge CB2 1RP
Bentley House, 200 Euston Road, London NW1 2DB
32 East 57th Street, New York, NY 10022, USA
296 Beaconsfield Parade, Middle Park, Melbourne 3206, Australia

Library of Congress catalogue card number: 72–89806

ISBN 0 521 20119 5 hard covers
ISBN 0 521 09784 3 paperback

First published 1973
Reprinted 1974, 1977

First printed in Great Britain
by Cox & Wyman Ltd, London, Fakenham and Reading
Reprinted in Great Britain by
Redwood Burn Limited, Trowbridge & Esher

Contents

1	Conceptual relativism	*page* 1
2	Wittgenstein and religious concepts	28
3	Commitment	43
4	Forms of life	64
5	The rationality of commitments	93
6	Relativism and disagreement	119
7	Rationality	138
	Bibliography	169
	Index	171

1

Conceptual relativism

Relativism and subjectivism

A fundamental distinction must be drawn between the way the world is and what we say about it, even if we all happen to agree. We could all be wrong. Some of the most important commitments we make in our life could be based on error. What is true and what we think is true need not coincide. This simple statement seems self-evident, since it merely draws attention to human fallibility in general, and our own in particular.

It might be salutary to remind ourselves of our fallibility if we felt certain about what to believe. In fact, however, many now would not only doubt that we can ever arrive at truth, but would doubt whether there is such a thing. We are faced with fundamental human disagreement not merely over what to believe, but over what would count in the first place as an adequate reason for belief. Morality and religion are notoriously areas where humanity seems to speak with many voices. Science seems by contrast to provide an example of a discipline where there are settled methods for ending disputes, and there exists an impressive unanimity of belief. Even here, however, the same problem can arise. What are we to say to somebody who will not accept the assumptions of Western science in the first place? And even the unanimity of scientists disappears when we approach the frontiers of knowledge and encounter the controversies of contemporary research.

Perhaps, then, it is not surprising that it is currently fashionable to decry the notion that certain things are simply *true*, and are therefore valid for all men whether they recognise the fact or not. Many people shrink from claiming that their moral or religious beliefs have this kind of truth and that those who reject the beliefs are mistaken. This hesitation may arise from a desire to be tolerant, from the fact of persistent disagreement in these areas, and also from the truism that no-one has a monopoly of truth. It can slip imperceptibly into the view that while one set of things may be true in one religion or one society, a different set may hold in another. Truth is then made to depend on what groups of people happen to believe. The possibility of false beliefs is ruled out, so that a whole community could not be judged mistaken. What its members believe is true for them, just as what we believe is true for us. Facts are then dependent on the way people think, and no room is left for the idea that things can be the case whether anyone thinks they are or not. In other words, the possibility of something being objectively the case is ruled out. Truth must always be considered *relative* to a society, whether it consists of the believers in a particular religion, the holders of a certain scientific theory, the members of one tribe, or any other identifiable grouping.

All this means that it is impossible to conceive of any kind of independent reality. Reality becomes merely what people think it is, and as different people have different conceptions of it, there must be different realities. However, to hold that there is no such thing as 'reality' but only realities seems itself to be an incoherent position. It is in effect to claim that it is objectively true that there are different realities and that they exist whether each person concerned with his particular world realises it or not. Thus the very denial of the possibility of something being independently or objectively real itself rests on the view that the various realities are objectively real. The incoherence can be shown in another way. If someone declares that truth is not objective but only relative to societies, he may very well claim 'there is no such thing as "objective truth"' or 'truth is relative to societies'. Both assertions, however, clearly purport to be objectively true, and are intended as truths about all societies. There would not be much point in the relativist uttering them if he did not wish to convince someone else of them. He thus has to accept that sentences which state his thesis are apparently inconsistent with it. He can always claim that the truth of his words is only relative to his own society, but as their whole point is to describe other societies as well, this just serves to emphasise the incoherence in the position.

The difficulty of stating relativism without lapsing into self-contradiction is not enough to counterbalance its undeniable attractions, and different versions of the theory will be forced on our attention in the course of this book. The term 'relativism' often seems to be used without any great precision, and it sometimes appears to be no more than a synonym of 'subjectivism'. The subjectivist holds that what I think is true is true for me and what you think is true is true for you. He is making truth relative to individuals rather than to groups of people. Protagoras is usually thought to have made the classic statement of the relativist position, but the views which he put forward in Athens in the fifth century B.C. seem to be much more those of the subjectivist as we have defined him. Protagoras maintained that man is the measure of all things. Plato quotes him as holding that anything 'is to me as it appears to me and is to you as it appears to you'.[1] This makes it clear that Protagoras is thinking in terms of each individual, rather than of societies. He is not saying that what is true in Egypt may not be true in Athens, but that what is true for Protagoras may not be true for Socrates or someone else.

Both relativism as applied to societies and subjectivism as applied to individuals are alike in what they deny, and this is presumably why the two are sometimes not distinguished. Neither allows for the logical possibility that the beliefs of an

[1] Plato, *Theaetetus* 152 A.

individual in the one case, or of a society in the other, can be judged by measuring them against anything external to the beliefs. The conception of something being the case apart from either a community or an individual thinking it is, is ruled out by both. Man effectively decides what is to count as true and what is to count as false. Truth is in the mind of the thinker, according to the subjectivist, or arises from the collective agreement of a society, according to the relativist. The objectivist, on the other hand, holds that truth is a goal which we aim at but do not necessarily reach.

By talking in terms of societies, the relativist does seem to allow some scope for beliefs to be mistaken or wrong, since *individuals* may be mistaken. They may make judgments which happen to go against the views of their society, and which as such may be false for that society. The individual would thus be subject to the standards of the society. Presumably the man who is out of step with his society has come to hold beliefs which are not shared by others in his community. This means that there is a disagreement in the society, which must be resolved by deciding what the majority thinks. There is clearly an oddity in deciding by ballot or similar means what is to be true, even if it is to be merely truth relative to a society. It may be said that it only appears odd because we are still bewitched by an objectivist view of truth. The point of the ballot, however, would be to ask what each man believes, or in other words what he thinks is *true* and it is obviously circular to use this as a basis for the definition of truth.

We could avoid this by asking people to predict in the ballot what the result of the ballot would be. This is not circular, although it may be idiotic. Even here, however, the incoherence of the situation is brought out when we consider what precisely we are supposed to predict. The only possible answer is that we must predict our own and other people's predictions. This must involve predicting our own and other people's predictions of our predictions ... and so on. It is certainly possible to predict the result of a ballot on a definite issue, but this merely emphasises that people have to have beliefs *before* the ballot.

The conclusion must be that once it is allowed that different people believe different things in a society, truth cannot be defined in terms of what that society thinks. Everyone in a society may unthinkingly accept the same beliefs, and this is particularly liable to happen in an unsophisticated society immune from outside influences. If, however, they begin to consider consciously what to believe, they cannot all look at each other simultaneously to see what the majority thinks. It must therefore be assumed that individual judgments about what is true precede questions about what most people think. Each individual must have some prior conception of what it is for something to be true, which is totally independent of what others happen to think. A relativistic view of truth appears to collapse at this point.

It may be argued that if only one or two question the established beliefs of a society, the beliefs of nearly all members of the society would still be true for the society as a whole. The minority is wrong and the majority right. The relativist then faces a difficulty: just because he maintains that a knowledge of the standards of a society is sufficient for knowing what is true (for that society), he has to agree that it is impossible to go further. He cannot accept what the current standards are and yet question whether they are right, or assert emphatically that they are mistaken. He can attach no meaning to such a procedure. Yet this seems to be what the lone rebel, the reformer, and even the prophet, are doing. The relativist can only allow that these men are mistaken about what the standards in a given society are; they cannot recognise the standards and still reject them.

Relativism and social anthropology

In the face of this criticism, a relativist might accept that in the last resort relativism reduces to subjectivism. He might agree that whatever influences may be present in a society, each person must fully make his own decision whether to accept them or not.

One popular form of relativism apparently manages to avoid this slide into total subjectivism. It does so by making reasoning as well as truth relative to groups or societies. Proponents of this position are usually very reluctant to be called relativists. Nevertheless, once it is stressed that different cultures have different concepts, and that their members see the world differently, it is no very great step to saying that there is no *right* way of seeing the world and that it is pure arrogance to assume that one's own society's understanding of things is the correct one. It thus becomes impossible to judge other cultures at all, since to do so we would have to rely on our own conception of what really is the case, and this is to beg the question as to who is right. What we are left with are separate ways of thinking about the world, or a particular part of it. There can be no neutral way of describing the world, against which every conceptual system can be measured. It is obvious that we can only describe the world by means of some conceptual scheme, and so it is logically impossible to step outside every conceptual system. (We shall consider later the vital question of what anyone is to count as a conceptual system.) The result is that we are apparently left imprisoned within our own system, unable to pass judgment on other systems without using our own. This is fine if ours enables us to think of reality as it is, while other systems give a false picture. Since, however, the adherents to each system are liable to think that theirs sets the standard of truth, an obvious compromise is to say that there is no such thing as truth when conceptual systems are being compared. Each system sets its own standard of truth, but is not itself the kind of thing which can be true or false. Such a position seems to be a paradigm case of relativism.

The same kind of problem arises whenever two fundamentally different sets of concepts appear to compete for our allegiance. It arises when we are faced with different religions, different moralities or different scientific theories. It arises when a Western scientist meets someone with a belief in magic. Most of all, of course, it arises when members of one culture meet members of such a radically different one that many of the concepts of the one culture fail to have any near equivalent in the other. It is not surprising that social anthropologists are often tempted by versions of what we might term 'conceptual relativism'. They may not explicitly espouse it or accept all its consequences, but their writings show considerable sympathy for the position. For instance, John Beattie writes:

Modern social anthropologists who are studying unfamiliar and 'unscientific' belief-systems ... do not proceed by framing the ideas they involve in formal propositions about reality, and then trying to conjecture how a reasonable man (that is, the anthropologist himself) could possibly have come to accept them. This was the Victorian approach. What we do today is to attempt to understand these beliefs in the whole context of the culture of which they are part.[1]

This may seem fairly innocuous at first sight. It is obviously dangerous to tear any assertion out of context and imagine that one can still fully understand it. Indeed, this kind of consideration prompts social anthropologists to go and live as one of the community they wish to study. Only then can they hope to get a proper grasp of the significance of certain ways of speaking and behaving. Beattie, however, is not just making this empirical point. He goes on to deny that systems

[1] Beattie, *Other Cultures*, p. 67.

of belief should be understood as making claims about 'reality'. They do not involve propositions which may be true or false. His 'contextual' approach leaves him with no way of appraising the beliefs of any cultures, and his only aim can be to understand them. He can never judge them, and would regard this as a strength of his position. He criticises the Victorians for thinking of other cultures as 'primitive' and inferior to their own, and remarks that 'childish' was one of their favourite adjectives when dealing with non-European cultures.[1] Certainly such Victorians may be accused of arrogance, but Beattie's position goes to the other extreme and in the end makes it impossible for any belief to be dismissed as superstitious or just mistaken. Rain-making ritual then has to be accepted on its own terms in just the same way as in other cultures weather-forecasting using 'advanced' technology has to be accepted on its terms. They are different, but we are left with no way of saying that one is better than the other. Even to say that scientific weather-forecasting is more successful or more accurate is to beg the question as to what should count as 'success' or 'accuracy'. The rain-maker might totally reject the Western scientific view on such matters, and might not be unduly worried when his efforts did not produce rain. He would doubtless be able to produce some explanation as to why they did not, however 'unscientific' it might be.

Beattie's approach makes us accept different conceptual systems as ultimate. Each sees the world in a different way, and so in a very real sense one cannot talk of 'the world'. There are many different worlds. Lévy-Bruhl similarly insisted that 'primitives live, think, feel, move and act in a world which in a great many ways does not coincide with ours'.[2] He enlarged on this by explaining: 'To the primitive mind, the seen and unseen worlds form but one, and there is

[1] *Ibid.* p. 65.
[2] Lévy-Bruhl, *Primitive Mentality*, p. 59.

therefore uninterrupted communication between what we call obvious reality and the mystic powers.'[1]

Once the notion of a reality independent of the way people think of it is given up, we can no longer talk of 'reality' but only 'realities'. To echo Protagoras, reality is to a community as it appears to that community. Beattie himself is tempted by this conclusion. He says:

Members of different cultures may see the world they live in very differently. And it is not just a matter of reaching different conclusions about the world from the 'same evidence'; the very evidence which is given to them as members of different cultures may be different. If in one sense all men everywhere inhabit the same world, in another and important sense they inhabit very different ones. And where these differences are culturally determined, social anthropologists are centrally interested in them.[2]

This last remark poses a major problem. How can the social anthropologist come to understand the differences? It first involves understanding the beliefs and practices of very alien cultures. This is always difficult, but without the concept of a reality independent of their beliefs, which their beliefs purport to be about, it seems to become logically impossible without becoming a participant in the culture concerned. If men in different cultures merely hold different beliefs about the same world, it is a fairly straightforward matter in principle (if sometimes difficult in practice) to find out what the equivalent beliefs in the various cultures are. If, however, they hold beliefs which are related to other beliefs in the same culture but to nothing external to it, nobody can grasp the point of any belief without setting it against its proper context in that society. Many beliefs may have no exact equivalents in other cultures, and indeed some cultures may be so unlike each other that there may appear to be no points of contact at all. In such a situation no-one can stand

[1] *Ibid.* p. 98.
[2] Beattie, *Other Cultures*, p. 75.

outside the society in question and hope to understand anything, since it would be impossible for its beliefs to be translated into terms which make sense in one's own society. The only path to understanding would be to live in the society concerned and begin to see things through their eyes.

This conclusion may be quite acceptable to social anthropologists and they have come to see the vital importance of field work. When we say that the only way to understand a society is to go and live in it, we are only emphasising what seems sound common-sense. It does, however, have the unwelcome result that only contemporary societies can be fully understood. No-one can go back in time to live in Ancient Greece, and so it appears to be impossible to understand the concepts current, say, in Athens in the fifth century B.C. Indeed, since Victorian England saw the world somewhat differently from present-day England, the present argument would suggest that it is logically impossible for an Englishman nowadays to gain a full understanding of how his grandparents thought. Further, since it is logically impossible for a parent to become his child, or *vice versa*, and since the world was in many respects a different place before the Second World War when many present-day parents were growing up, it might be argued that it is logically impossible for a parent to understand the way his child thinks and looks at the world. The completely different experience each has had means, it might be said, that neither will see things in precisely the same way, and that the concepts of the post-war generation will be markedly different from those of the preceding generation.

This whole thesis clearly depends on a particular view of the nature of concepts. In particular, it regards the circumstances in which concepts are learnt as determining the nature of those concepts. The result could be, if this view were to be pressed too far, that each person would be imprisoned in his own private world, since each person might be said to acquire his concepts in different circumstances.

It is significant that Margaret Mead, the anthropologist, does put forward an account which is remarkably similar to the view we are examining. She does this in a study of the so-called 'generation gap', and says:

All of us who grew up before World War II are pioneers, immigrants in time who have left behind our familiar worlds to live in a new age under conditions that are different from any we have known. Our thinking still binds us to the past – to the world as it existed in our childhood and youth. Born and bred before the electronic revolution, most of us do not realise what it means.[1]

She believes that 'once the fact of a deep, new, unprecedented world-wide generation gap is firmly established, in the minds of both the young and the old, communication can be established again'.[2] In other words, the elders have to realise the young think differently, and that their own concepts create a barrier to understanding. She continues: 'As long as an adult thinks that he ... can ... invoke his own youth to understand the youth before him then he is lost.' At least, it seems, she does not think that mutual understanding is logically impossible. It is just exceedingly difficult. The elders are in a very real way like social anthropologists doing field work. Like them, they must work hard to understand fully the strange culture they find themselves in.

The snag is that for them and the social anthropologist understanding should only be the first step. The social anthropologist will also want to relate features in the society he is studying to features in other societies, and to compare the different cultures. Moreover, he will presumably look for points of contact between his own society and the one he is studying. Similarly the older generation will wish to compare the concepts of the younger generation with their own

[1] Mead, *Culture and Commitment*, p. 73.
[2] *Ibid.* p. 79.

and even try to translate them more or less adequately into their own terms. Margaret Mead seems to maintain that this is logically impossible, since the pre-war world and this world are too unalike. What she is in fact putting forward is a form of conceptual relativism based on generations rather than on geographically separated societies.

Conceptual relativists do not have to hold that it is always logically impossible to acquire a different set of concepts, provided that they are still current in a society. We can always go and live in the society concerned. We may indeed even be able to gain through its writings a glimmering of understanding of the concepts of a society which has disappeared. There is, though, an apparent difference between, on the one hand, going to live amongst Samoans and learning to think like a Samoan and, on the other, merely studying the literature of ancient Athens. One can only try to think *as if* one was an Athenian. One never actually becomes one. There is the same difficulty about the 'generation gap', as seen by Margaret Mead. (Whether there actually is such a gap is an empirical matter and is not our present concern.) It is possible for an older person to behave *as if* he was young and learn to see things *as if* he was born after the Second World War, but he cannot make either true. Is the difference a real one? An anthropologist, imbued with the values of the Western world cannot, it may be suggested, actually *become* a Samoan (even discounting the obvious fact that he cannot acquire Samoan parentage). He may live as if he was Samoan, and pretend to see things through Samoan eyes, but the fact is that he also sees everything through Western scientific eyes.

Does any of this matter? Whether a man has actually become a Samoan, or merely thinks as if he were one, he still has a grasp of Samoan concepts. The difficulty is that the non-Samoan does not seem to be committed to the Samoan conceptual scheme, in the way that the Samoan is. The anthropologist has not forgotten his own culture, any more than the parent trying to understand his rebellious offspring has forgotten his own way of looking at the world. As long as the anthropologist remains a Western scientist, he can never hope to see things in exactly the same way as a native of the society he is studying. He can try to see things through the native's eyes, but unless he gives up his scientific outlook altogether he will never be able to think like the native. At best he will achieve the schizophrenic position of being able to switch from the native's outlook to his own and back again.

Beattie sees that this difficulty arises from his position. If one can only understand a society by becoming a participant in it, the fact that one is already committed to the beliefs of another society does seem to be a hindrance to full participation and therefore to full understanding. He says:

We can enter in some degree into other people's ways of thought and we can attain some understanding of their beliefs and values, but we can never see things *exactly* as they see them. If we did, we should have ceased to be members of our own culture and gone over to theirs. But we can go a long way towards achieving this kind of comprehension, while still retaining a foothold in our own world. Perhaps social anthropology's chief claim to respect is that it has achieved some success in doing this.[1]

Beattie might fairly be accused of begging the question with the last sentence. It is the very possibility of social anthropology which is at issue. If full understanding of a society is only possible for someone who is totally committed to the society, the task of the social anthropologist is an impossible one. Either he remains sufficiently detached to retain his scientific viewpoint, and therefore fails to gain a full understanding of the society, or he wholeheartedly commits himself to the society and stops being an anthropologist.

[1] Beattie, *Other Cultures*, p. 76.

Beattie clearly thinks, despite the relativistic overtones, that a fairly adequate understanding is possible for the anthropologist. It seems, however, to be the kind of understanding of concepts which comes simply from learning how to use them. At this level, the social anthropologist is no better off than any member of the society he is studying. Whether he can translate its concepts into terms his compatriots would understand, and whether he can compare different societies in any useful way is another matter. It is not just that this is always a difficult and challenging task. The problem is rather that by the way it wishes to make sharp divisions between societies and divide their concepts up into self-contained compartments, conceptual relativism seems to make any comparison between societies impossible.

Conceptual relativism

If the members of different societies live in 'different worlds' and do not merely have varying and conflicting beliefs about the same reality, there will not necessarily be any point of contact between the concepts of one society and those of another. If different societies are dealing with the same world, it is possible in principle to examine how differently they describe the same things. All that is necessary is to see what members of the respective societies say when confronted with a specified situation, such as a cat on a mat. The words of one group can then be regarded as a translation of the words of the other. If the assumption concerning the objectivity of what they describe is removed, there can be no justification for comparing what they say, because they may be talking about totally different things. In these circumstances, instead of their concepts depending on the composition of the world, the concepts determine the composition. Different concepts, therefore, mean a different world, so that what the world is like is relative to a conceptual system and the language of the system.

Winch is an example of a philosopher treading the relativist path in considering the status of the social sciences. How far he is actually a relativist is a matter of debate, but he certainly refuses to separate 'reality' from language, so that language actually seems to determine what is real. Even an objectivist, of course, would admit that there is a close link between a language and what is regarded as real. A language expresses a community's beliefs about reality. The objectivist, however, would still wish to insist that 'reality' existed apart from people's beliefs, and that their beliefs could be mistaken. An essential function of language, he would maintain, is to concern itself with what is actually the case. Its business is to attempt to communicate *truth*. Winch will have none of this. He says:

Reality is not what gives language sense. What is real and what is unreal shows itself *in* the sense that language has. Further, both the distinction between the real and the unreal and the concept of agreement with reality themselves belong to our language.[1]

It follows that different languages cannot be thought of as different attempts to describe the same reality. 'Reality' is made relative to a language, and if different languages portray 'the world' differently, then there must be different worlds.

If one accepts this conclusion, one is remorselessly driven to unpalatable consequences. The result of granting that 'the world' or 'reality' cannot be conceived as independent of all conceptual schemes is that there is no reason to suppose that what the peoples of very different communities see as the world is similar in any way. Unfortunately, however, this supposition is absolutely necessary before any translation or comparison between the languages of different societies can

[1] Winch, 'Understanding a Primitive Society', in *Religion and Understanding*, ed. D. Z. Phillips, p. 13.

take place. Without it, the situation would be like one where the inhabitants of two planets which differed fundamentally in their nature met each other and tried to communicate. So few things (if any) would be matters of common experience that their respective languages would hardly ever run parallel. In this latter case it might be agreed that the languages could still be about things which would be open to inspection by visitors to the planet in question and that at least some of the language would be learnt fairly easily (for instance, by ostensive definition). The possibility of communication does then exist. It follows, however, from the position of the conceptual relativist that this kind of learning is impossible, since the world of each culture cannot be observed before one has acquired the culture. It is putting the cart before the horse to imagine that one can inspect the world so as to understand the culture in the way that one could observe the nature of a planet so as to understand the language of its inhabitants. The latter still depends on the objectivist assumption that what we see is the same as what the inhabitants of the planet see.

The objectivist must of course accept that it is impossible to argue outside all conceptual frameworks. If, however, I use the presuppositions of one particular framework in argument, I can, it will seem, always be fairly criticised for begging the question. Why should *that* framework be the correct one? Each can only be justified using its own terms, and that seems merely to be saying it cannot be justified. If a Western medical researcher meets an African witch-doctor, the former's talk of 'viruses' and the 'evidence' he produces will not be likely to impress the latter. The whole argument can be represented as a basic clash between two different ways of looking at the world, or, to put it in more clearly relativistic terms, between two different worlds. The objectivist need not deny that two very different conceptual systems are involved, although he will reject the notion of different worlds, and will be content to see the disagreement as one between different outlooks on the one world. If the conflict is seen like this, both sides clearly cannot be right. Both may be wrong but it is also possible that one side is right, and the other mistaken. The Western scientist *may* be right about the cause of certain diseases, and his appeals to other tenets of Western science *may* equally reflect things as they are. The point is that even if this was the situation, or even if the opposite was true and the witch-doctor was correct in his claim that an illness was caused by an evil spirit, the scientist (or the witch-doctor) could still be accused of begging the question. Because he keeps to his own conceptual scheme, he is apparently indulging in a vicious circularity which his opponents are justified in not accepting. This argument holds even if his concepts correctly reflect reality as it is, and his opponents are grossly mistaken. He can apparently be blamed for refusing to see things in other than his own terms even when his terms are the right ones.

The argument about begging the question can be applied to any position, when different conceptions of the world are at issue. Indeed, to point out that someone is only thinking in his own terms seems to say something fairly trivial. A Western scientist is obviously going to think like a Western scientist. His arguments, so far from begging the question, merely reflect his belief that Western science is *right* – or, at least, nearer the truth than any alternative. However, the argument against him still apparently works, even if his belief is justified. In other words, the accusation about begging the question itself presupposes that the objectivist is wrong, and that a belief that one's conceptual scheme reflects reality must be mistaken. The argument is only a good one *if* relativism is correct, and that is what is at issue. The argument itself begs the question.

Consider the case of someone who refuses to accept that

the earth is not flat. He has a ready answer for anyone who produces evidence to show that the earth is round (such as ships disappearing over the horizon, or photographs of earth taken from the moon). The flat-earther can always say that such 'evidence' is not the kind of thing *he* would count as evidence, and that anyone who thinks the earth is round is ignoring what *he* counts as important; whether the 'evidence' produced is really evidence is precisely what is at issue, and his opponent is merely begging the question. It is obvious that no evidence could be produced to show that the earth is round which would satisfy such a flat-earther. There are two possibilities left in the face of such an apparently insoluble disagreement. The first is to accept the relativist position that there is more than one way of ultimately looking at the matter. One may be a committed flat-earther or a committed round-earther and our view of what is to count as evidence stems from these commitments. The second course is to accept that the round-earther has made his case, and that the flat-earther is just *wrong*. The mere fact that what the round-earther said was not acceptable to the flat-earther does not in any way suggest that he is assuming the truth of what he is trying to prove. It could merely show that the flat-earther is so pigheaded that he cannot recognise the truth when it is presented to him.

The significant thing is that the mere existence of an unresolved disagreement still leaves the relativist-objectivist controversy wide open. Just because neither accepts the other's presuppositions, we should not assume *a priori* that one set of presuppositions cannot be right. Even to be ready to describe the situation as the clash of different conceptual systems itself leads to conceptual relativism, and more than the simple existence of a disagreement is needed to justify this.

Another impetus to conceptual relativism is provided by the suggestion that there is a close connection between the meaning of a concept and the conditions under which it is learnt. K. Baier says of someone being taught the concept of pain: 'Since he learns the word on the occasions when he feels something he wants to stop ... the very meaning of "a pain" will be "something which I dislike".'[1] I have argued elsewhere[2] that this is a very unsatisfactory analysis of the concept of pain. Baier is right about the conditions necessary for teaching the concept, but it does not necessarily follow from the fact that we can only learn the meaning of 'pain' when dislike of the sensation is being expressed that 'pain' can only refer to unpleasant sensations. Once we have learnt the concept, we may have occasion to apply it in strange but legitimate ways. If this is right, two people (or different groups) who share the same concept may find themselves in fundamental disagreement about how to apply it. If it is wrong, such basic disagreement must be seen to result only in the holding of different concepts, conceptual relativism and the total breakdown of communication.

This all becomes particularly important in the case of moral concepts. R. W. Beardsmore wishes to tie their meaning very closely to the conditions in which they are learnt. Because the holders of a particular moral outlook learn 'right' and 'wrong' in connection with particular things, Beardsmore assumes that the meaning of 'right' and 'wrong' is connected with them. He says:

It is *within a particular moral code* that we find the framework of agreement. For instance, we have seen that within a Catholic morality men agree in the significance which they attach to considerations like suicide and adultery, and it is from such considerations that their use of the terms 'right' and 'wrong' draws its meaning. In saying this, I am of course rejecting ... any account according to which these terms have the same meaning for all of us.[3]

[1] Baier, *The Moral Point of View*, p. 275.
[2] Trigg, *Pain and Emotion*.
[3] Beardsmore, *Moral Reasoning*, p. 121.

The meaning of 'right' and 'wrong', therefore, is thought by Beardsmore to vary according to what is actually termed right or wrong. The words then get their meaning from the conditions in which they are learnt, and these will be different for a Catholic and non-Catholic (particularly if the latter is not a Christian at all). Beardsmore would admit that there is considerable room for overlap here. Clearly a Catholic and non-Catholic would agree in many of their applications of the word 'wrong'. Beardsmore might maintain that this would allow us to say that they could understand each other, but it could equally well be said that as the concepts of the Catholic and of the non-Catholic were each applied to different, though overlapping, sets, the concepts were significantly different. As a result, each man would be talking past the other, instead of to him. When a Catholic said abortion was wrong, and a humanist said it was not wrong, neither would mean precisely the same by 'wrong' and they could not be thought to be contradicting each other. Whether he would agree with this or not, Beardsmore would certainly accept that if a primitive tribe applied 'moral' language to a completely different set of things from us, there could be no point of contact at all between our moral concepts and theirs. Once again we have arrived at a version of conceptual relativism.

It is a great mistake to confuse the meaning of a concept with the occasions on which it is learnt. This can be seen quite simply from the fact that once a concept is learnt it can be applied in completely new situations which are in some ways very unlike those in which we may have first grasped the concept. Even though an adherent to a particular moral code may have learnt the word 'wrong' by applying it to a specific set of things, he should then be able to go on to apply it, if he wishes, to some situation which he has never met before. If 'wrong' was just the word to be applied to certain specified things, this would be impossible. An inability to make moral judgments about anything he had not previously encountered would hardly be evidence that he really knew what it was for something to be wrong. It would merely suggest an ability to repeat what he had been told parrot-fashion. Someone who was taught what 'red' was by being shown London Transport buses and British pillar-boxes could hardly be said to have grasped the concept of red if he was never willing to call anything else 'red'. There would be the added difficulty that someone who was taught what 'red' was with the use of different concepts would apparently have a different concept. In short, 'red' does not even in part mean 'the colour of a pillar-box', even though the concept may be taught by means of pillar-boxes. If the Post Office suddenly painted all the boxes yellow, our concept of red would not change at all (though we could no longer teach it by means of pillar-boxes).

There is no contradiction in supposing that none of the things by means of which we were taught 'red' are red any more (because they have all been repainted some other colour). Similarly, it is perfectly feasible that we no longer wish to call wrong any of the things which we were taught as children were wrong, and yet that we still have the same concept of wrong. Our moral views have changed and we now *disagree* with what we were taught. We can simply deny now that a certain thing is wrong even though we once thought it was, and this is significant. We recognise that we can contradict what we would previously have said, although this would be impossible if we were now operating with a different concept. Our concept of wrong does not change merely because we change our mind about what is wrong. Obviously if someone has such a complete change of heart that there seems to be no contact at all between his present views and his previous ones, we would want some assurance that he does retain the same concept. If he eagerly attempts to do everything which he says is wrong, we would have grave doubts. If, however, he makes a deliberate effort not to do what he says is wrong, shows remorse when he fails to practise what he preaches, and so on, it should become clear that his moral views, and not his concepts, have changed. Beardsmore makes any change in moral outlook depend on a conceptual change. Moral concepts are thus made relative to moral codes.

Relativism and conceptual relativism

Beardsmore's emphasis on the importance of moral codes suggests that more than the meaning of moral concepts may be involved. If suicide is regarded in totally different ways in two codes, one may well begin to wonder whether the concept of suicide is the same in both. A possible explanation why it is regarded as wrong in one but not in another may be that 'it' is not regarded in the same way in each. D. Z. Phillips takes this line of argument to its logical conclusion when he writes:

> If I hear that one of my neighbours has killed another neighbour's child, given that he is sane, my condemnation is immediate ... But if I hear that some remote tribe practises child sacrifice, what then? I do not know what sacrifice means for the tribe in question. What would it mean to say I condemned it when the 'it' refers to something I know nothing about? If I did condemn it, I would be condemning murder. But murder is not child sacrifice.[1]

This is relativism with a vengeance. It suggests that nineteenth-century missionaries had no right to tell Fijians that cannibalism was wrong, on the grounds that no-one outside the society could possibly know how they regarded eating people. To us it might be eating people, but to them it might be something quite different. Phillips' view is simply that no practice can be condemned from outside the culture of which

[1] Phillips, *Faith and Philosophical Enquiry*, p. 237.

it is a part, no matter what that practice might involve. Only by joining the society (and presumably taking part in child sacrifice, or cannibalism) could one begin to understand. Such a course might appear to be morally repugnant, but the repugnance we feel might be said to be merely a sign of our personal commitment to the standards of our own society. This reflects a line of argument which can always be deployed when there is such basic disagreement that neither side will accept the assumptions of the other. If one side still insists that it is right, what is this assertion really doing? It in no way alters the situation, since the other side will most certainly not accept it. Thus, it will be said, my assertion that I am right is merely an expression of my own commitment. This all depends on a tough-minded empiricist approach which refuses to acknowledge that anything can be valid or true for somebody, if he does not acknowledge this to be so. The logical outcome of all this is an extreme subjectivism where nothing can be regarded as true for somebody until he sees that it is, and when, as a result, no distinction can be made between his thinking something true and it being true. 'Truth' becomes a consequence of belief or commitment and not a reason for it.

If the whole argument is removed from the individual level to the level of conceptual systems, it may be said that a condemnation of other systems is merely a reiteration of our collective commitment to *our* system. The argument then becomes merely another version of the accusation of begging the question, which, as we saw is itself merely an assertion of conceptual relativism.

We remarked earlier that those who espouse versions of 'conceptual relativism' are reluctant to be called relativists. For instance, Phillips and Mounce carefully distinguish their position from that of Protagoras, even if his position is interpreted not as a subjectivist one, but as an assertion that, as they say, 'truth and goodness are determined, not by the opinions of individual men but by the conventions which they create'.[1] They assert:

Although Protagoras was correct in maintaining that the agreement of the majority plays a role in making it possible to have conceptions of truth and falsity, he was wrong in what he took the role to be. On Protagoras' view, the agreement of the majority is not merely a necessary condition for the notions of truth and falsity: it is itself *the measure* of truth and falsity.[2]

Phillips and Mounce wish to follow Wittgenstein in his emphasis on the preconditions for the holding of concepts. This is a different question from the question what is actually to be regarded as true or false. The latter can only be asked amongst those who share enough concepts to be able to communicate with each other. However, ordinary relativistic theories and conceptual relativism both emphasise the importance of human agreement. The former are merely concerned with agreement over what is true, whereas conceptual relativists go further and stress that basic agreement is a necessary condition for our holding the same concepts. If everyone disagreed about everything, we could never even begin to teach concepts. Phillips and Mounce say: 'If the majority of people could never reach agreement in colour judgments, then colour judgments would cease to be made.'[3] It follows that when different judgments are consistently made by different groups of people there is a difference in concepts.

Conceptual relativism appears more extreme than ordinary relativism, since it is concerned with meaning and not just with truth. The two must always be closely linked, but conceptual relativists make meaning their prior claim. They hold that what I count as true in my language may not even be able to be described in yours. Translation becomes

[1] Phillips and Mounce, *Moral Practices*, p. 61.
[2] *Ibid.* p. 63.
[3] *Ibid.* p. 62.

impossible in principle. Truth is made to depend on concepts, and as concepts are relative to 'forms of life', truth must be as well.

'Ordinary' relativism which makes truth dependent on the conventions which arise out of human agreement, may allow that different societies, or groups of people have different views about what is true and are still able to understand each other. Since it rules out the possibility of there being any reality independent of the beliefs, how is this understanding to be achieved? As long as there is agreement about what is to be counted as true, there is clearly no problem, but where there is consistent and basic disagreement, there seems to be no way of formulating what is at issue. If one group of people call 'red' a totally different set of objects from those we call 'red', we might expect that they are just using the word differently, and we might think we could look at the way they used it to see what they mean. This itself presupposes an objectivist view of the world, by imagining that we can in principle pick out the same differences between objects as others do. It even presupposes that objects are the same for them and for us. A relativist can make neither assumption, but has to accept that if a group of people use a word in what seems an odd way, we cannot hope to know what they are talking about. We must just recognise that they think in a way which we are logically barred from understanding. This is clearly to espouse conceptual relativism. In other words, conceptual relativism is not just one form of relativism, but is itself the logical outcome of any form of it. If the world is so different for different groups that they can be said to live in different worlds, their language is bound to reflect their different experience. Whether differences in their view of reality are thought to lead to different concepts, or differences in concept are thought to lead to different views of what is the case, the result is clearly the same. It is a chicken and egg situation and conceptual relativists are only drawing the moral for meaning which is already implicit in the ordinary relativist's treatment of truth.

Any theory which emphasises above all else the importance of some kind of agreement inevitably leads to relativism. It suggests that truth is not dependent on what is the case, but on what people think is the case. As there are many divergent views about what is the case, there is no way, given an emphasis on agreement, of establishing what is so independently of the different agreements people come to. If separate groups fail to agree, the only possible recourse which this view has, is to refuse to talk of truth outside the framework of their agreement. The question of truth then becomes an internal matter in the different systems. This is currently a popular way of dealing with truth. There is, however, no question of the system itself being true or not. As a result, there can be no grounds for committing oneself to the system. One either is committed or not, and recognition of what is true must follow a commitment. The question of relativism, and the problem of there being ultimate commitments which are arbitrary and outside the scope of reason thus become inextricably entwined.

2

Wittgenstein and religious concepts

Wittgenstein's view of religious belief

The slide into relativism occurs in a variety of contexts. For example, there has been a great deal of discussion in recent years about the relationship between religious belief and 'straightforward' factual belief. Does the belief that there is a God have the same logical status as, say, the belief that there are elephants in Africa? Is it, on the other hand, so radically different from all factual belief that it is wrong even to talk of anything counting for or against religious belief? In this debate the shadow of logical positivism still looms large, with its demand that religious utterances be capable of empirical verification if they are to have any meaning. Apologists of religion have become very chary of assimilating religious beliefs to beliefs of an everyday kind. It is easy to check the truth of a belief about elephants, whereas it seems impossible to settle the question of the existence of God. Many have then fallen into the temptation of insulating religious belief from awkward questions about its truth or its meaningfulness, by saying that religious language has its own criteria of meaning and truth.

Anything which distinguishes religious belief from other kinds of belief will clearly tend to support those who wish to champion the view that religious language has its own rules and that these mark it off from other uses of language. It will enable them to maintain that religious belief, as it is expressed in language, cannot be judged by criteria appropriate to other 'forms of life' (to use a term from Wittgenstein which we shall examine later). We must therefore examine how peculiar statements of religious belief seem when compared with other kinds of statement.

Ethical statements such as 'That is right' are often contrasted with plain statements of fact such as 'That is a pillar-box'. Whereas no course of action necessarily follows from the fact that an object is a pillar-box, it is inconsistent to say that an action is the right one and not to see that therefore it should be done. Ethical statements typically guide action in a way in which many statements do not. To recognise that an action is wrong, I have to commit myself to trying to avoid it. I do not have to commit myself to posting a letter if I recognise that an object is a pillar-box. While I can be indifferent to many states of affairs which might be talked about, my use of moral language logically precludes any indifference. Its action-guiding force is part of its meaning.

Much the same kind of thing is claimed for religious language. It looks as if some statements logically cannot be made by someone who is indifferent to their religious significance. Could someone agree that Christ rose from the dead but say 'So what?' Is not that the kind of belief which must affect a man's whole life, once it is accepted? There certainly seems something odd about treating it as an historical fact amongst other historical facts, which has as little relevance to the way someone lives his life today as the murder of Julius Caesar. It seems to carry with it the necessity of a personal commitment to Christianity. Indeed, an assertion that Christ rose from the dead seems actually to be a part of such a commitment.

These kinds of consideration weighed heavily with Wittgenstein.[1] He was particularly concerned with the role which religious belief played in a man's life, and saw that what distinguished someone's religious belief from his other beliefs was its enormous influence on every part of his life. Religious belief requires total commitment, and seems totally unlike the disinterested entertaining of a scientific

[1] Wittgenstein, *Lectures and Conversations on Aesthetics, Psychology and Religious Belief*, ed. C. Barrett.

hypothesis. It seems to go far beyond any evidence which might justify it, and it is remarkably impervious to criticism and argument. Wittgenstein takes as an example[1] someone who has a belief in the Last Judgment and makes this belief guide his life. He regulates his whole life 'foregoing pleasures, always appealing to this picture'. Wittgenstein comments: 'This in one sense must be called the firmest of all beliefs, because the man risks things on account of it which he could not do on things which are far better established for him.' A religious belief like this is distinguished by Wittgenstein from a factual belief based on evidence. He maintains that such a belief would not influence my way of life at all. He says:

Suppose, for instance, we knew people who foresaw the future: made forecasts for years and years ahead: and they described some sort of a Judgment Day. Queerly enough, even if there were such a thing, and even if it were more convincing than I have described, belief in this happening wouldn't be at all a religious belief.[2]

Wittgenstein comments that if I had to forgo all pleasures because of such a forecast, the best scientific evidence would not be enough to influence me. Scientific evidence is not the kind of thing which will guide me in the way I live. Wittgenstein says the same of historical evidence. Even if there is watertight evidence in favour of the historicity of the events portrayed in the Gospels, Wittgenstein claims that this is insufficient. In fact, he would maintain that the notion of evidence is out of place here. He says: 'It has been said a thousand times by intelligent people that indubitability is not enough in this case. Even if there is as much evidence as for Napoleon. Because the indubitability wouldn't be enough to make me change my whole life.'[3]

As a result, Wittgenstein thinks that Christianity 'doesn't

---

[1] Wittgenstein, *Aesthetics, Psychology and Religious Belief*, p. 53.
[2] *Ibid.* p. 56.
[3] *Ibid.* p. 57.

rest on a historic basis in the sense that the ordinary belief in
historic facts could serve as a foundation'. Belief in certain
facts might be the basis for a further belief about an historic
event. I might, for example, base beliefs about the Emperor
Tiberius on firm historical evidence such as coins and in-
scriptions. Wittgenstein denies that a belief in the events of
the New Testament could be of the same logical type. My
beliefs about Tiberius are based firmly on evidence. Wittgenstein claims that religious beliefs may even fly in the face
of evidence.

Wittgenstein does make explicit a view which is implicit
in all he says. He claims of belief in the historic basis of
Christianity: 'Here we have a belief in historic facts different
from a belief in ordinary historic facts. Even, they are not
treated as historical, empirical propositions.'[1] In effect, he
claims that statements about Christ are, for a believer,
logically different from statements about Tiberius. The latter
can be treated as true or false, proved or disproved. They
can be more or less firmly based on evidence. They will be
accepted or rejected in a disinterested way. I shall not change
my way of life if I change my views about the character of
Tiberius. Statements about Christ, however, have, according
to Wittgenstein, rather the role of pictures which are constantly in my thoughts. He says: 'Here, an enormous difference would be between those people for whom the picture
is constantly in the foreground, and the others who just
didn't use it at all.'[2] Doubt has no place in this model.
Wittgenstein comments: 'Those people who had faith didn't
apply the doubt which would ordinarily apply to *any*
historical proposition.'

For Wittgenstein, commitment logically precedes rather
than follows the entertaining by a Christian of a proposition
about Christ. Commitment, he feels, cannot follow the

[1] *Ibid.* p. 57.
[2] *Ibid.* p. 56.

piecing together of historical evidence. He considers that it is neither reasonable nor unreasonable to believe. It is not a matter of reason at all. Once we are committed Christians, certain pictures play a powerful role in our life. If we are not committed, the pictures do not play that role. In fact, Wittgenstein says, in that kind of situation, 'I think differently, in a different way. I say different things to myself. I have different pictures.' As a result, it is impossible for a non-religious person to contradict a religious person. The one does not have the thoughts and the pictures the other has. They are, as it were, operating on different wave-lengths. Wittgenstein sees that if you cannot contradict a religious person, that may mean that you do not understand him. He says: 'I don't know whether to say they understand one another or not.'

It is important to realise in all this that Wittgenstein is not conducting an attack on religious belief. He is not saying that what a religious man believes is meaningless. That would involve imputing a standard of meaningfulness from some other realm of discourse and applying it to religion. This is precisely the kind of approach Wittgenstein would attack. The most he is saying is that religious propositions seem meaningless to the unbeliever. This can also work the other way. The believer may not understand the non-religious man. It follows from this that neither can say that the other is mistaken. Wittgenstein says: 'Whether a thing is a blunder or not – it is a blunder in a particular system. Just as something is a blunder in a particular game and not in another.'[1] Wittgenstein stresses that you cannot use the rules of one system to judge another. Just because it is an infringement of the rules of soccer to run with the ball, it does not follow that a rugby player is doing anything wrong if he does the same thing. Wittgenstein applies this to different kinds of reasoning. He could hold that a blunder in scientific reason-

[1] Wittgenstein, *Aesthetics, Psychology and Religious Belief*, p. 59.

ing need not be a blunder in religious reasoning. Different rules apply.

'Reductionism'

Much of what Wittgenstein says about the difference in character of religious statements from non-religious ones acts as a powerful antidote to those philosophers who in effect have tried to apply the standards of experimental science to religion. They have been too ready to assume that because statements about God are unscientific, in the sense that they are incapable of proof or disproof by ordinary scientific means, they must be meaningless. Wittgenstein, on the other hand, equates the meaning of a word with the way it is used. On this view, to describe the role which a concept plays in people's lives is to elucidate the concept fully. It is not surprising that his view results in religious statements being linked logically to a commitment. It is only a short step from this to saying that the meaning of such statements *is* the commitment. Braithwaite takes this line in his well-known lecture on 'An Empiricist's View of Religious Belief', although his analysis is in some respects significantly different from Wittgenstein's. For Braithwaite, the 'stories' of a religion are mere psychological aids to moral commitment and are contingently related to it. Something else might do as well. Wittgenstein thinks that the pictures we entertain are much more important in determining the nature of the commitment. He says: 'The whole *weight* may be in the picture.'[1]

Braithwaite takes the meaning of a statement as being given by the way it is used and asserts: 'The primary use of religious assertion is to announce allegiance to a set of moral principles.'[2] As has often been pointed out, the average

---

[1] *Ibid.* p. 72.

[2] Braithwaite, 'An Empiricist's View of the Nature of Religious Belief', in *Christian Ethics and Contemporary Philosophy* (ed. I. T. Ramsey), p. 63.

believer would not accept this kind of analysis of what he says. He thinks he is saying something about God and Christ, and he would deny that he is merely talking about himself and his outlook on life. Some philosophers would claim that this was irrelevant. They would say that the task of philosophical reduction which Braithwaite and others undertake is a matter of meta-theology. It is an analysis of theological statements and is not itself a theological statement. It can only be an elucidation of religious language. It cannot be the fundamental challenge to religion which it is sometimes taken to be. G. H. Hughes draws a parallel with other branches of philosophy and says:

The phenomenalist in epistemology or the emotivist in ethics is likely to be unmoved by the fact (if it is a fact) that most users of material object language or moral language are unsympathetic to his account. And rightly, surely?

Was then the fluttering in certain Christian dovecotes which followed the delivery of Braithwaite's lecture due to a sheer confusion between theology and meta-theology, between philosophical reduction and outright denial?[1]

An analysis of the way a statement is used ought not to put into question the statement itself. The two are on different levels. The phenomenalist is not denying the existence of material objects. He is trying to show that our statements about material objects can be translated into statements about actual and possible sense data. Even if we agree with his analysis, we shall not stop talking about chairs and tables. We can still discuss and settle the question how many chairs there are in the room. Many contemporary analyses of theological language may seem at first sight to be doing a similar job. They certainly attempt to demonstrate how statements about God should be translated into statements about something else. It may be our commitment to

[1] Hughes, Review of *Religious Belief* by C. B. Martin, *Australian Journal of Philosophy* XL (1962), 217.

a particular morality, our 'ultimate concern', loving personal relationships, or anything which removes the necessity of talking about the transcendent. Obviously the empiricist will find it more congenial to pay attention to our commitment and its influence in our lives than to attempt to include God within an empirical framework. The question is whether it is possible to do justice to religion with this kind of approach.

The phenomenalist can still talk about chairs with a non-phenomenalist. Can a reductionist theologian talk of God with a non-reductionist? An immediate difficulty is what is to count as reductionism. Anyone giving an analysis of what Christians mean when they say certain things is likely to resist the suggestion that he is reducing their talk of God to talk of something else. He may very well accuse those who allege reductionism of begging the question as to what religious statements really mean. However, both the phenomenalist and his opponent can discuss whether a chair is large or small, heavy or light, comfortable or uncomfortable and so on, and the fact that someone holds one philosophical position rather than another ought not to restrict what can be said. Once one replaces talk of God with talk of human commitment, it becomes very difficult to say some of the things which are ordinarily said of God. This is clearly because the emphasis is shifted from what is objectively the case, whether or not anyone recognises it, to the way men happen to think or behave. It is a characteristic ploy in the philosophy of religion to make out that references to anything transcendental or miraculous are really about men and their attitudes. It is surely legitimate to call this a 'reductionist' policy.

In Christianity it seems to be a tautology that God created the universe, but clearly human commitment to God did not create it. Once one has adopted a reductionist theology and has restricted one's attention to the influence of religion on men's lives, it becomes impossible to talk of a personal God or a Creator. A statement such as 'God created the universe' can no longer be treated as true (or false), if this is understood as saying something about the origins of the universe. It has to be translated into some statement about the attitudes of those who believe it. For example, D. Z. Phillips says: 'To see the world as God's creation is to see meaning in life. This meaningfulness remains untouched by the evil in the world because it is not arrived at by an inference from it.'[1]

Statements which appear to be about God are in this way shown to be about believers. What people believe is thought to be less important than the influence of their beliefs on them. Certainly a result of seeing the world as God's creation could be to find meaning in life and live accordingly, but it is misleading to identify the two. The question would naturally arise whether theists were right in finding meaning in life or whether they were under an illusion. The believer would say there was meaning *because* the world was created by God. He would be appealing to what he would consider to be a fact. He would not be saying that there was meaning because there was meaning. This, however, is what reductionists would have to understand him to be saying. A belief in God as Creator is different from a mere determination, which may be totally misplaced, to see meaning in life. If the belief is correct it provides the justification for finding life meaningful.

It will, of course, be immediately objected that no sense can be given to the notion that the belief could be correct or incorrect. This, we would be told, is to suppose that there are standards of correctness and incorrectness which can be applied to religious belief from outside. It is to ignore everything that Wittgenstein says. We shall be returning to this point. Here it is enough to realise what great violence this approach does to the average believer's view of his faith. An

[1] Phillips, *The Concept of Prayer*, p. 97.

affirmation of belief in God as 'Maker of heaven and earth' can no longer be understood as an assertion of a literal truth about a Being existing independently apart from the world of space and time. Nothing can be thought of as counting for or against the statement.

It is not enough to say that to talk of a Creator is to be influenced in one's life by a certain picture, or to entertain a certain story. Braithwaite, in maintaining the latter, says that it is not necessary for the man who makes a religious assertion to believe in the truth of the story involved in the assertion.[1] In other words, the ordinary believer is being told that he is wrong in thinking that what he believes to be true is true. His beliefs are not really beliefs after all. They are the frills on a commitment to a certain way of life, instead of the justification for it. What is offered is not so much a philosophical analysis of religious belief as a denial of its truth. It is cold comfort to the believer to be told that this does not mean his beliefs are false. He is unlikely to be very happy to find that they are so utterly different from ordinary beliefs that they are neither true nor false.

Belief in God

The emphasis on commitment and the dismissal of the notion of reasons for it derives in part from the contrast drawn with science. Religious belief, it is thought, is radically different from the entertaining of a scientific hypothesis. This is not intended to be a criticism of religion, since Wittgenstein's point is that science and religion just involve different systems of thought, and that what counts as 'truth' in each is radically different. He says that we do not talk about hypothesis, or about high probability, in religious contexts.[2] There are not, he says, those who say about the Resurrection 'Well,

[1] Braithwaite, 'An Empiricist's View', p. 67.
[2] Wittgenstein, *Aesthetics, Psychology and Religious Belief*, p. 57.

possibly'.[1] One is either committed or one is not. As a result, it is natural that what seems important is the influence which the Resurrection has on people's lives. Its place in their thoughts is regarded as crucial, and inevitably questions about its historicity can come to be disregarded as irrelevant. This whole approach reaches its logical conclusion in what is said by a writer on aesthetics:

Why, to put the point incisively if painfully, should we demand a birth certificate of Jesus of Nazareth any more than of Oedipus or Buddha or Hamlet? Why can we not live and grow in these beings imaginatively, without feeling any nagging guilt because we cannot recite their social security numbers? Are they not in human terms much more important than they would be if they were merely literal and historical?[2]

Underlying this, and much of what Wittgenstein and others say, is the assumption that one cannot give mere intellectual assent to many statements which are important for religion. That would be to treat them in a way the scientist approaches his subject matter. The corollary of the view that religious statements play the kind of role which great art plays in human life is that they do not have to be regarded as true to be influential. The events in Shakespeare's *Julius Caesar*, and the way they are portrayed, may move us. It is irrelevant to ask if they happened just like that. Anyone who thought that the correct response to *Julius Caesar* was an investigation into the historicity of the events portrayed would be sadly mistaken. Should the events in the New Testament be regarded any differently? Is intellectual assent important? This is another way of asking if they are the kind of events which can be thought of as objectively true or false, and which can justify a religious commitment. In fact the same questions arise with all religious statements, and, above all, with the most basic one, 'God exists'.

[1] *Ibid.* p. 56.
[2] D. N. Morgan, 'Must Art Tell the Truth?', *Journal of Aesthetics and Art Criticism* XXVI (1967) p. 26.

Many philosophers nowadays deliberately ignore the traditional arguments for the existence of God, and any attempts to 'prove' the existence of God. Their reason is not that they find the arguments inconclusive. They feel that to argue for the existence of God at all is to treat it as a scientific hypothesis; belief that God exists is then a propositional belief which may or may not be followed by any commitment. The trouble with this, which such philosophers point out, is that it is difficult to see what a belief 'that God exists' comes to without any commitment and without a belief *in* God. To those who emphasise the role of religion in life, the mere entertainment of a religious proposition in a neutral way seems impossible. N. Malcolm stresses this in his article on 'Psychological Explanation of Religious Belief'. He considers it logically, and not merely psychologically, impossible to believe that God exists and have no 'affective attitude' towards Him. He asks:

Would a belief that he exists, if it were completely non-affective really be a belief that he exists? Would it be anything at all? What is the 'form of life' into which it would enter? What difference would it make whether anyone did or did not have this belief?[1]

No philosopher worries about the difference a belief that there are elephants in Africa could make to a person. Much of Malcolm's concern arises from the fact that he considers a religious belief such as that God exists to be of a radically different kind from beliefs for which there is a settled procedure to decide whether they are correct. He says: 'When it comes to adducing evidence for or against the existence of God, there is no agreed-upon framework.'[2] He claims that we do not know what a good reason for belief in God would look like. To support this he points out that people seem to make up the rules according to their inclinations as

[1] Malcolm, 'Psychological Explanation of Religious Belief', in *Faith and the Philosophers* (ed. J. Hick), p. 107.
[2] *Ibid.* p. 109.

they go along, in arguments about the existence of God. He says: 'Since there are different indications, there is no agreed-upon right or wrong in this kind of reasoning.'[1] Similarly Wittgenstein in *Philosophical Investigations*[2] emphasises that there must be agreement in judgments as a pre-condition of language being a means of communication. People cannot share their concepts if they do different things with them. It follows that people must agree about the application of a concept. Wittgenstein tries to show, using pain as an example, that it is impossible to hold a concept with a private element which cannot be shared. He insists that there must be public, agreed criteria. It follows that the concept of God cannot gain currency without agreement about its application. It looks from this as if it must be impossible for any but believers to talk of God. This seems to cut out all possibility of arguing about the existence of God, if it is assumed that there is a simple choice between being committed and not being committed. Either one already believes in Him, or one cannot talk of Him at all.

Malcolm does not think that the belief that God exists has any genuine content. He thinks the whole notion of reasons for such a belief misplaced, and he concentrates on how belief in God influences a man. In this way he can put on one side any question about the rationality of the belief, and instead just accept the belief as a fact. He shows how such a belief can 'get a grip on the world' now that there is no question of its verification or falsification. He says: 'The man who believes that his sins will be forgiven if he is truly repentant might thereby be saved from despair . . . the belief makes a great difference to his action and feeling.'[3]

Once again, we see an abandonment of any notion that in religious belief anything is believed to be objectively *true*.

[1] *Ibid.* p. 108.
[2] § 242.
[3] Malcolm, 'Psychological Explanation of Religious Belief', p. 110.

My belief becomes not much more than a way of looking at the world. It will make a difference to my life, as it will govern the way I react to situations. It involves a determination to be hopeful and not despairing, to feel dependent and not self-sufficient, to find meaning in life, and so on. It does not include the entertainment of any proposition which can be shown to be true or false, outside the system of religious belief, of which it is a part.

We shall examine in a later chapter Wittgenstein's views on the nature of concepts and 'forms of life', which lie behind all this. It is sufficient at the moment to question the validity of the radical break which is alleged between scientific and religious belief. This centres on the idea that scientific belief involves a detachment which is impossible with any genuine religious belief. D. Z. Phillips says:

To say 'This is the true God' is to believe in Him and worship Him. I can say 'This theory is true, but I couldn't care less about it' and there is nothing odd in what I say. On the other hand, if I say 'This is the true God, but I couldn't care less' it is difficult to know what this could mean. Belief in the true God is not like belief in a true theory.[1]

The phrase 'belief in God' is a slippery one. To say 'I believe in God' may be a disinterested acknowledgment of a fact, but it seems more naturally used as a confession of faith and commitment. Does someone saying 'it is true that God exists' necessarily have to be committed in any way? If he is not, we are told, he is not saying anything. Either the words are given a sense by the role they play in his life, or they have no sense. Without this philosophical presupposition, however, does it follow that there is a clear logical distinction between religious beliefs and scientific beliefs?

Genuine religion does seem to demand a realisation that one's beliefs about God are relevant to the way one regards the world and the way one lives one's life. Someone who says, 'It is true that God exists, but so what?' does puzzle us.

[1] Phillips, The Concept of Prayer, p. 149.

He does not seem to understand the importance of what he has acknowledged. It is possible, however, for someone to become convinced intellectually that there is a God. He might even have treated the statement 'God exists' as a scientific hypothesis. Many philosophers have been accused of doing just that. The religious person may feel that what the philosophers are doing has nothing to do with religion. This is not the point. It looks as if a belief that God exists could be intelligibly described without any commitment being involved. D. Z. Phillips is right in thinking that the religious response to the realisation that 'this is the true God' is to worship. The correct religious response, however, need not be the only reaction which is logically possible. Indeed apathy or detachment need not be the only non-religious responses. It does not seem self-contradictory to imagine someone accepting fully that there is a God, and repudiating Him completely. This is presumably the position the Devil holds in Christian theology. On a mundane level, not every-one who rejects the demands of Christianity need be an atheist or an agnostic. It does not seem at all unintelligible (even if it may be irrational) that someone should prefer to live an utterly selfish life, whilst still accepting that there is a God to call him to account. He may genuinely fear the wrath of God, while remaining totally impenitent.

The view that one has only to acknowledge God to wor-ship Him seems a gross simplification. Phillips ran together the acceptance of the proposition that there is a God with the natural religious response, and emphasised the latter at the expense of the former. The two are logically distinct, and difficulties about the meaningfulness of 'God exists' should not blind us to that. The fact that acceptance of proofs for the existence of God, or of historical evidence about Christ, may only result in a detached intellectual acknowledgment of God does not mean that they are necessarily irrelevant for the purpose of religious commitment. It would seem irrational for a man who accepted the truth of Christianity not to attempt to live his life accordingly. Irrationality, however, is different from logical impossibility. It must be recognised that there are two distinct parts in religious commitment, the acceptance of certain propositions as true and, as a result, a religious response, expressed in both worship and action.

3

Commitment

The nature of commitment

All commitments must involve beliefs which may turn out to be true or false. It is not adequate to maintain that the beliefs only have a truth which is relative to the society, conceptual system, or whatever is in question. Such a system could involve beliefs which are only true within it, but ultimately we must come to the question of commitment to the system. That commitment must be based on beliefs which are themselves external to the system. They could not be internal to it without a vicious circularity. I could not be committed to a system *because* of my belief in something which is only true relative to that system. In fact, the only alternative is to admit that commitments to systems must be regarded as 'ultimate' in some sense, and that they do not involve any form of propositional belief. Although this notion of an 'ultimate commitment', which is in principle unjustifiable, is attractive to many, it involves a basic misunderstanding of the nature of commitment.

I can never be just 'committed'. I must always be committed to something or somebody. If I commit myself to God, I base my life on my belief that there is a God. The fact that our commitments can never be 'free-floating' but are always directed means that there must be a propositional element lurking behind every commitment. I must have some conception of what I am committed to. As a result, I cannot be committed to a God, if I believe that there is no God. Similarly, no-one could be a committed Marxist if he believed that Marx was basically mistaken. The fact that I am committed to some cause shows that I believe that the cause is a good one and worth supporting. It also shows that I believe it to be important in some way. In other words, there is what some philosophers call an 'evaluative' element in commitment. I cannot commit myself to something I believe to be utterly trivial or totally bad. It may be both, but in so far as I commit myself to it of my own accord I cannot realise that it is either. Someone who was a committed Liberal would not agree that the Liberal party was a total irrelevance in modern British politics, or that any influence it had was all to the detriment of the country. This is a matter of logic, and not an empirical generalisation about Liberals.

In any sphere the fact of commitment logically entails certain beliefs and precludes certain others. One must believe in the truth of what one is committed to. Supporters of the Flat-Earth Society must if they are committed flat-earthers believe that the earth is flat. They must also believe that it is important and desirable to have a society to put their view forward. It is possible for someone to give support to such a society without really believing that the earth is flat, but such a person could hardly be called a 'committed flat-earther'. He may be in the society for a laugh, or may even be a committed anti-flat-earther, dedicated to undermining the society from within. It is also possible for someone to believe that the earth is flat without being a committed flat-earther. He just accepts the views of the flat-earthers as true without bothering to act on them. In the same way one can be a Christian without being a committed one. One could believe that Jesus Christ was the Son of God while letting the belief have only a marginal influence in one's life.

Any commitment, it seems, depends on two distinct elements. It presupposes certain beliefs and also involves a personal dedication to the actions implied by them. Each element can occur without the other, but if someone is truly committed, both elements will be present. Someone who devotes his life to a cause which he does not believe in cannot be genuinely committed, whatever the reasons for his hypocrisy. Similarly, no-one who holds certain beliefs and fails to make any effort to act on them can be thought in any way committed. Mere intellectual assent to Marx's doctrine does not make a man a committed Marxist.

What I am committed to determines the nature of my commitment. If my beliefs change, my commitment must. A man cannot be called a committed Christian if he holds no distinctively Christian belief. He may act in what appears to be a Christian manner. He may be a better man than many Christians. These are not, however, sufficient grounds for calling him a Christian. He may believe that he ought to love his fellow men, and could therefore be said to be committed to living a life of love. If he holds no explicitly Christian belief, as a matter of definition he cannot be termed a committed Christian. Similarly someone may strongly support some welfare programme advocated by socialists. If he sincerely repudiates the socialist principles underlying the policy, he could not be called a committed socialist, even if at least for a time, his actions were indistinguishable from those of genuine socialists.

It may be objected that all this puts too much emphasis on propositional belief. It could be pointed out that the best way of finding out what the man believes is to see what he does. What sense can be given to the suggestion that two people who behave in the same way consistently over a period of time nevertheless have different beliefs and therefore different commitments? Even if the two claim to believe different things, our objector might say, their actions show that their commitments are really the same. This view accepts that any commitment depends on some propositional belief, but claims that actions speak louder than words. What a man does is a more reliable guide to what propositions he accepts than what he says.

There must be some truth in this objection. The mere fact of a man saying that he believes something would not be enough to convince us that he is not lying or deceiving himself. Someone who says he believes that there is a God and does not allow this belief to influence his way of life at all may seem almost an atheist. We have, however, already given examples of situations where it seems intelligible to talk of an acknowledgment of God without any commitment. Most plausible, perhaps, are those cases where there is undoubted fear of God and of the consequences of disobeying Him, coupled with a determination to go on pursuing selfish pleasures. Even though there is no commitment we have very good reason there to talk of a belief that there is a God. The line between the atheist and the man who accepts that there is a God but remains totally indifferent, may be very difficult to draw. It does not follow that it cannot in principle be drawn.

Belief and commitment

The importance of the propositional element in any commitment cannot be over-emphasised. If there is none, or if acceptance of it cannot be distinguished logically from becoming committed, reasoned argument becomes impossible. When my commitment cannot be separated from my beliefs, any questioning of my beliefs becomes a direct onslaught on my commitments. If my commitment to what I believe to be true is distinguished from my beliefs, it seems that I can argue unemotionally about my beliefs whilst still remaining committed. When I change my beliefs, my commitment must change, since I cannot be committed to what I recognise as false. Questioning my beliefs and even doubting their truth need not necessarily weaken my commitment. If, on the other hand, acceptance of their truth is *identified* with my commitment, it follows that every time I become dubious about one of my beliefs, my commitment becomes less strong. Indeed, in such a case, doubting my beliefs would be precisely the same as becoming less committed. There could be no such thing as intellectual doubt.

Wittgenstein maintained that commitment logically pre-cedes the entertainment of religious stories or pictures. Since he would deny that such pictures could be either true or false, it is probably misleading to talk at all of his view of religious 'propositions'. He really denied that there could be such things. His complete emphasis was on the fact of com-mitment. Either one was committed or one was not. No reasons could be given for or against any commitment. It just happened.

Any approach of this kind must run into difficulties pre-cisely because it ignores the crucial importance of the pro-positional element. Not everyone is committed to the same thing. There are many different kinds of commitments and they all cannot be right. Many conflict with each other. How can we decide between them? Wittgenstein faced this problem in connection with ethics. He says:

Suppose someone says 'One of the ethical systems must be the right one – or nearer to the right one.' Well, suppose I say Christian ethics is the right one. Then I am making a judgment of value. It amounts to *adopting* Christian ethics.[1]

Wittgenstein makes no distinction between judging which of several rival ethical systems is correct and adopting it. He explicitly differentiates between this situation and one where we decide which of rival physical theories is the true one. A physical theory could be verified or falsified according to the way it corresponds or conflicts with the physical world. He would claim that as there was nothing against which an ethical system can be judged, no sense can be given to talking of it as 'the right one', if one is talking of more than one's

[1] Quoted by R. Rhees, *Phil. Rev.* LXXIV (1965), 24.

commitment. The system is merely either adopted or rejected. Wittgenstein would say the same of conflicting religions.

There is more than a whiff of subjectivism about all this, Wittgenstein, however, did not mean that each man's ethics or his religion were true for him, or right for him. He says: 'That could only mean that each judges as he does.' He did not hold that all systems were equally right. He says curtly: 'That means nothing.' Wittgenstein thought that to talk of 'right' or 'wrong', 'true' or 'false' in connection with religion or with ethics would be to admit that there was after all a propositional element in religion and ethical commitment. If one did use any of these words they could only be understood as expressing an acceptance or rejection of a commitment.

In the same context, Wittgenstein claims: 'If I say, "Although I believe that so and so is good I may be wrong": this says no more than that what I assert may be denied.' He has to say this if he is going to deny the presence of any propositional element. It should, however, be clear that thinking I may be wrong is totally different from thinking that what I assert may be denied. I may already be aware that many men do deny it, and for this very reason wonder which of us is right. I would not be concerned with whether I may one day myself deny what I now assert and sometime give up my present commitment. My interest would not lie in what other men now think or in what I will one day think myself. I would want to know whether so and so really *is* good. I would accept that my reasons for thinking it good may not be valid. Wittgenstein's claim that all talk of the rightness or wrongness of commitments is really only talk of the commitments themselves removes all possibility of explaining what such a worry is about.

If Wittgenstein is right, there is no possibility of ever criticising the basic beliefs and commitments of others in the fields of morals and religion. Questions in an area such as that of logic can be discussed and difficulties resolved because there are standards of correctness to which we can appeal. Wittgenstein would deny that there are any such criteria in ethics or religion which we can apply to show that others are mistaken or confused. The most he would say about other people's religious views which he did not share was that he would never believe what they believed. This would not be a criticism of them but a mere statement of fact. He would deny that he was in a position to criticise, any more than he was in a position to applaud their beliefs. He merely did not share them and as a result was very likely unable to understand them properly.

The view that there are no standards which can help us decide between different religions and moralities makes Wittgenstein reject what we have called the 'propositional element' in basic commitments to them. He does not believe that when a religion or a morality as such is in question, there could be any claims to truth which could be understood and perhaps challenged by those who were not similarly committed. The commitment generates its own standards. As a result, he believes that it is only possible to be wrong in relation to a particular system of belief. It is possible to be wrong about the nature of God from a Christian standpoint. It is not possible to be wrong (or right) about the existence of God. One is either committed to Him or not. If you can only be wrong in relation to a system of belief, and you can only be judged according to the standards of that system, Wittgenstein considers that you will only be understood by those who are adherents to it. This means that only believers can use the word 'God'.

Commitment and meaning

The view that in the field of religion believers and un-
believers cannot, as a matter of logic, discuss basic questions
together looks odd. Many atheists would say they could
understand the claims of the Christian religion, and would
also say they were false. Many Christians would think they
understood everything an atheist said against Christianity,
and in spite of his objections would still feel they had good
reasons for believing the Christian religion to be true. Often,
Christians are only too conscious of the force of what an
atheist might say (for example, about the presence of
suffering in the world). They might feel they could answer
the points made, but they could still accept them as a
challenge to their faith which has to be met. Wittgenstein's
view of the self-contained nature of different commitments
makes this common experience incomprehensible. How
could any attack on religion shake anyone's faith, if believers
could not even understand it? To put the same argument
round the other way, how could any agnostic or atheist ever
give pause for thought about the claims of religion if they
are completely unintelligible to him? Yet many do, and
some become Christians, knowing full well what they are
becoming committed to. If Wittgenstein was right, nobody
could ever understand what Christianity was before they
became Christians.

D. Z. Phillips accepts Wittgenstein's position and carries it
to its logical conclusion when he suggests that even ex-
Christians would not understand what Christianity was
about. He says:

If a people lost their belief in God, belief in God is not intelligible but
false for them, but unintelligible. To no longer believe in God is not to
disbelieve one thing among many of the same kind, but to see no sense

in *anything* of that kind. What has become meaningless is not some feature of a form of life, but a form of life as such.[1]

It is certainly true that religion may not mean anything any longer to such people, in the sense that they no longer see any point in it. This is very different from finding it meaningless in the sense of not understanding it. Religion may now mean nothing to them because they have come to the conclusion that its claims are false, and this presupposes that they do understand the claims. Such people may feel that it is senseless being religious when religion is based on falsehood. However, thinking that it is senseless (or foolish) to utter religious statements is different from finding religious statements in themselves senseless (or meaningless).

Many things which meant a lot fifty years ago mean little or nothing to the modern generation. Patriotism nowadays means nothing to some, although it is still far from meaningless to many. This is not to say that some people do not understand the meaning of the word 'patriotism' while others do. Some just do not see the point of loving one's country and even despise those that do, while others still think it is important. Even if nobody believed in patriotism that would not immediately entail that the *word* became meaningless, even though what it stood for no longer had any meaning for people.

It could still be used in describing historical periods when patriotism was important, just as we might talk of the age of chivalry, even though chivalry may now seem dead. In fact, the meaning of a word should be distinguished from questions about how much meaning is still possessed by what the word refers to. Words such as 'senseless' and 'meaningless' can be dangerously misleading. I do not consider everything which I find meaningless to be literally nonsense. Seeing no point in a way of life or a system of belief is different from

[1] Phillips, *Faith and Philosophical Enquiry*, p. 46.

finding a string of words to be nonsense (for instance, 'red grins the dogs over'). There is no contradiction in both understanding a description of a certain practice, and finding the practice itself pointless and meaningless. It is possible to understand a full description of a game of golf and still see no point in playing the game. The various actions of the golfers may be perfectly intelligible, while the activity as a whole may seem totally senseless. In the same way, religious commitment could seem pointless to people who nevertheless could understand what beliefs were being held.

D. Z. Phillips makes a similar transition from one sense of 'meaning' to another when he talks of someone from a non-religious background who asks, 'How do I begin to understand what is meant by prayer?' Phillips says: 'If the question is asked from a desire to be able to pray, the questioner has some idea of prayer, and prayer has begun to mean something to him. If, on the other hand, the questioner cannot make any sense of prayer, his question is extremely difficult to answer.'[1]

There is a confusion here between 'what is meant by prayer' and 'what prayer means to someone'. It is possible to explain what prayer is without delving into the psychological question of what prayer means to particular individuals. What prayer is and what it means to me are two different issues. I can understand the meaning of the word 'prayer' and understand what people do when they pray, without seeing any point in the practice. I can grasp the sense of 'prayer' without seeing any sense in praying. It may be that to understand fully what prayer is, I have to know the role it plays in people's lives. Prayer, however, does not have to be important to me, for me to see that it is important to others. It may even be true that one cannot wholly appreciate what prayer is, if one has never prayed, just as perhaps someone who has never been in love can never fully

[1] Phillips, *The Concept of Prayer*, p. 60.

appreciate what that involves. These are not conceptual questions. Whether I pray or not need not affect the way I use the word 'prayer'. Confirmed bachelors can still talk wistfully of 'love'.

The possibility of justification and criticism

According to Wittgenstein, our basic religious or moral commitments can make no claim to truth. The only way to adjudicate between them is for us to adopt one and reject the others. We can never tell someone who does not share our commitment that he is wrong. It seems, therefore, that a Christian ought not to say that his religion is true. Wittgenstein would point out that there is no agreed criterion of correctness for religions. He denies that any commitment entails a belief that certain things are true.

It is important to realise just how great a change in our view of religion is being proposed. Religious believers have usually thought that they were making large claims about the nature of the universe and the nature of man, which involved the rejection of other possible world views. Even when they could not establish some of their assertions by reason alone and talked of the necessity of faith, they were not abandoning any claim to truth. Faith may have gone beyond the evidence, and even sometimes apparently against it, but it was always faith in a God, who existed independently of man's thinking of Him. God was the ultimate truth and if He was a figment of man's imagination, man's faith was in reality totally unfounded and to be discarded. Faith involved the belief that even if man's reason was inadequate when dealing with the infinite and the transcendent, commitment to God was justified and reasonable. Faith involved the assurance that because this is God's world anything (such as the presence of evil in the world) which seemed to suggest that there was no God was in principle explicable as part of

God's providence, even if man was unable to explain it
himself.

Wittgenstein's rejection of the role of reason in religious
belief has nothing to do with this traditional Christian view
of faith. He is not saying that religious belief is a matter of
faith rather than reason, or that it is 'supra-rational'. When
he says[1] that religious belief should not be thought reasonable
or unreasonable it is a mistake to think that he is saying that
such belief goes beyond reason but not against it. To suggest
this would be to accept that religious belief could be thought
of as *true*. Wittgenstein, however, would stress that any
reference to the truth or falsity of religious belief was as misplaced as the reasonable-unreasonable dichotomy. He would
stress that different religions constitute different forms of life
with different conceptual systems. Each provides its own
criteria of truth, and it is impossible to stand outside them
all and adjudicate between them. One would by definition
be left with no standards by which to judge.

Wittgenstein does use the word faith[2] in connection with
religious belief. He points out that different words, such as
'faith' and 'dogma', are used for religious beliefs in contrast
with other beliefs. He also says (in a passage already quoted)
that people with faith don't apply the doubt to the historic
basis of Christianity which would ordinarily apply to any
historical propositions. Such references to 'faith' might
suggest that Wittgenstein is emphasising faith at the expense
of reason in a fairly traditional manner. It is clear from the
context that he is thinking of faith merely as a commitment
to a way of life. He would deny that it involved belief in the
truth of any propositions. The very fact that Wittgenstein
thinks faith and doubt are incompatible is significant. If faith
is merely commitment without factual belief, doubt can only
be a wavering in that commitment. Genuine faith and doubt

[1] Wittgenstein, *Aesthetics, Psychology and Religious Belief*, p. 58.
[2] *Ibid.* p. 57.

must then clash. If I doubt, I am that much less committed (although Wittgenstein's assumption that commitment is an all or nothing affair makes it difficult for him to allow a place for doubt at all). If, on the other hand, faith is thought of as at least a combination of commitment and a belief that certain things are true, it seems possible to have continuing faith in the face of doubt. This is much more in accord with traditional conceptions of faith.

I can remain committed while my beliefs are being challenged. If my doubt reaches the point where I lose my beliefs, it is true that I must lose my faith. I cannot have faith in anything which I am certain is false or in anybody who I am sure is merely a character from legend. On the opposite side, faith does not imply certainty. It is much more a determination to remain committed in spite of apparent difficulties. Although it must involve the belief that the difficulties do not provide genuine obstacles to faith, if the faith is to be rational, faith can exist in spite of seeming facts as well as because of them. There is no contradiction in my facing up to the possibility that my beliefs may be mistaken, while in the meantime holding firmly to my faith. I can be totally committed and at the same time admit that I might be wrong. I am however basing my life on the assumption that I am not.

Wittgenstein completely rejects the idea of a commitment being right or wrong, justified or unjustified. His reluctance to allow that any basic commitment can leave room for doubt stems from this. If I cannot be wrong, I cannot worry that I might be. One major result is that such commitments must be immune from criticism. Some philosophers and theologians welcome this conclusion. They are happy to ignore the fact that if nothing can, even in principle, count against religious belief, nothing can count in its favour. Instead, they are at great pains to fence off religious belief from anything extraneous. Nothing, they claim, which is said by scientists or historians can be relevant to religious commitment. They insure themselves against any possibility that historians might one day find evidence which suggests that the events reported in the New Testament are fictional, or that a scientific discovery might tell against a theistic view of the world.

Tillich makes some effort to emphasise that faith can be called 'true' if it is concerned with 'the really ultimate'. The whole tenor of his theology, however, is subjectivist and it is never clear how much sense can be given to talk of 'the really ultimate' when it is separated from the state of ultimate concern in man. He says: 'From the subjective side one must say that faith is true if it adequately expresses an ultimate concern. From the objective side one must say that faith is true if its context is the really ultimate.'[1]

It looks as if 'the really ultimate' is not much more than that which adequately expresses an ultimate concern. Certainly, Tillich assumes that the two must coincide. He asserts: 'The question of faith is not Moses or Jesus or Mohammed: the question is: Who expresses most adequately one's ultimate concern.'[2] In other words, questions of the truth of different religions can be reduced to what looks suspiciously like a psychological matter. If one is concerned with something which is not truly ultimate, Tillich thinks that the consequence is what he calls 'existential disappointment'.[3] This does little to suggest that religion need be anything more than a satisfying illusion. Even Tillich's differentiation between the subjective and the objective side of the act of faith begins to look somewhat unconvincing on closer examination. He says: 'This distinction is very important, but not ultimately so, for the one side cannot be without the other. There is no faith without a content toward which

[1] Tillich, *Dynamics of Faith*, p. 96.
[2] *Ibid.* p. 66.
[3] *Ibid.* p. 12.

it is directed. There is always something meant in the act of faith.'[1]

In other words, faith, in common with many mental states, needs an 'object'.[2] I must have faith in something or somebody, just as, when I am afraid, I must have an object of my fear. I cannot just fear. My fear can be at something which is in fact totally imaginary. The fact that people are afraid of ghosts does not prove that there are such things. It merely shows that they believe there are. Even if the 'object' of my fear does exist, my fear may still be unjustified. I might be afraid of a real cow but that does not make cows dangerous. Tillich's emphasis of the 'objective' side of faith does nothing to show that a person's faith may not be misplaced. The fact that someone has to have faith *in x* does not prove that his faith in *x* is justified, or even that it exists. Tillich's 'objective' side of faith is still firmly subjective.

Despite his use of the word 'true' in connection with faith, Tillich cannot distinguish between justifiable commitment and satisfying illusion. He joins the happy band who wish to protect religion from science and history. He asserts that whatever scientific progress is made, faith has no need to 'continue its retreat'. He claims that scientific truth and the truth of faith do not belong to the same dimension of meaning.[3] Similarly he turns to history and says: 'The truth of faith cannot be made dependent on the historical truth of the stories and legends in which faith has expressed itself. It is disastrous distortion of the meaning of faith to identify it with the belief in the historical validity of the Biblical stories.'[4]

Like Wittgenstein, Tillich is so preoccupied with the element of commitment in faith that he ignores the element

[1] *Ibid.* p. 10.
[2] See Trigg, *Pain and Emotion*, pp. 9ff.
[3] Tillich, *Dynamics of Faith*, p. 81.
[4] *Ibid.* p. 87.

of propositional belief. Very few would wish to *identify* faith with belief in the historicity of, say, the life of Christ. Clearly assent to certain assertions about Christ does not amount to faith. It is an essential *part* of faith in Christ. The fact that faith is more than factual belief does not mean that it does not involve it. If I have faith in Christ I must believe that He is more than a product of somebody's imagination. I must believe that He did live and that there are good reasons for my committing myself to Him. Because Christ is an historical figure, historical questions cannot be irrelevant to Christianity. To think that it does not matter whether Christ actually existed or whether His life and character are portrayed accurately by the New Testament is to say that it does not matter if Christianity is an illusion.

Like Wittgenstein, Tillich accepts that it is logically impossible for someone to criticise another man's commitment when he does not share it. If he does share it, then of course there would be no point. Tillich says:

If a Protestant observes a Catholic praying before a picture of the Virgin, he remains observer, unable to state whether the faith of the observed is valid or not. If he is a Catholic, he may join the observed in the same act of faith. There is no criterion by which faith can be judged from outside the correlation of faith.[1]

Either one is committed to *x* or one is not, and that, it seems, is all that can be said. Nothing can count for or against a commitment. It is worth noting that, unlike Wittgenstein, Tillich does not take this to heart, but is quite ready himself to criticise what he regards as an example of 'idolatrous faith', on the grounds that its holders are not concerned with the 'truly ultimate'.

Theologians such as Tillich protect Christianity from criticism at a high price. If all traditional claims to truth are jettisoned, one result may be total vacuity. This is a constant danger for religious belief when faced with criticism. It is

[1] Tillich, *Dynamics of Faith*, p. 59.

very easy to accept the criticism and qualify the belief. This can result in what Flew described in a famous phrase as 'the death by a thousand qualifications'. There is, however, an equal and opposite danger which is produced by the quest for logical invulnerability. Even if intelligible claims are being made within a system of belief, the fact that such systems are considered immune from criticism means in effect that they must all be considered of equal worth. It becomes impossible to distinguish reasonable belief from illusion and superstition.

This is also a weakness in Wittgenstein's conception of 'forms of life'. Any religion, however bizarre, has to be accepted as constituting a 'form of life'. It seems to Wittgenstein sufficient to say 'this language-game is played'.[1] No judgment can be passed beyond our personal commitment to, or rejection of, that particular religion. By implication the concept of superstition is denied any application. No distinction can be made between a faith which may go beyond reason, but does not go against it, and the beliefs of extreme religious sects. The latter often seem wild and irrational, and involve claims which run counter to the agreed findings of archaeology and history. They are liable to make predictions about the exact timing of the end of the world, and still to cling to their commitment when their predictions are proved wrong. They would, however, presumably form a distinct community of language-users with a single 'form of life'. Within the sect, certain statements would be regarded as correct, and others would be ruled out as incorrect. Are we to be told that we cannot appeal to normal historical and scientific criteria to say that their commitments are based on beliefs which are simply *false*?

This objection can be put in a more extreme way by pointing out that it is perfectly possible for a community to share a commitment based on beliefs which are logically

[1] Wittgenstein, *Philosophical Investigations*, § 654.

incoherent. Indeed, Christianity itself is often attacked because it involves a belief in an omnipotent and loving God, who allows evil and suffering. This is an attempt to show that the Christian conception of God is incoherent, because it attributes contradictory characteristics to Him. Christians may be able to defend themselves against this criticism, but the point is that it is incumbent on them to do so. It is highly unsatisfactory for them to say that because the Christian religion with its distinctive ways of talking exists, one must either accept its criteria of meaningfulness or fail to understand it. According to this one could never simply say that Christian belief is muddled and incoherent and therefore *ought to be* rejected.

Winch, following Wittgenstein, maintains: 'Criteria of logic . . . are only intelligible in the context of ways of living or modes of social life. It follows that one cannot apply criteria of logic to modes of social life as such.'[1] He suggests that religion is one such mode of life, and science another. He continues: 'We cannot sensibly say that either the practice of science itself or that of religion is illogical or logical: both are non-logical.' I shall later question more closely the notion of a 'mode of life' or 'form of life'. 'Religion' covers a multitude of modes of life, many of them in competition with each other. Either each religion provides its own criteria of intelligibility and can never be criticised by an outsider, or a particular religion can be judged from the outside. If the former, the result is that all religion is lumped together. No distinction is made between the rantings of extreme sects, blatant superstition, dangerous delusion, and the claims of more orthodox religion. If, however, any particular religion can be justifiably criticised, it is logically possible that *all* religions are muddled or false. Either all religions are to be protected from the criticisms which many of them obviously deserve, or all must be subject to searching examination.

[1] Winch, *The Idea of a Social Science*, p. 100.

Winch certainly appears to be on safe ground in suggesting that the practice of religion is non-logical. This is partly because 'religion' is such a vague term that until the claims of a particular religion are examined the question of illogicality can hardly arise. He also helps his case by concentrating on practices rather than on the religious beliefs which are inextricably involved in any religious commitment. A religious practice cannot properly exist without a framework of belief. It becomes an empty ceremony, almost a charade. While practices might not seem to involve logical questions even if they appear pointless, beliefs are certainly subject to the need for consistency. In addition, in contrast with beliefs, practices are not the kind of things which can be true or false.

Once the notion of there being a justification for accepting one religion rather than another is discarded, all questions of objective truth and falsity, and all distinctions between genuine religion and superstition, have to be swept aside. Commitments to different religions have each to be regarded as ultimate. Nothing more can be said about them. It is interesting to note how an analogous situation can occur in moral philosophy, even when ethics are separated totally from religion. R. M. Hare builds up a whole moral theory on an individual's ultimate commitment to a basic moral principle. His views are in many ways very different from those of Winch and others following Wittgenstein. He is not putting forward any general doctrine about the nature of concepts and their place in the life of a community. He is instead dealing with questions concerning the *individual*'s moral commitment. Even talk of modes of life cannot remove the possibility of an individual putting the question 'Why should I accept this mode of life?' In his denial of the possibility of giving a rational justification for certain commitments, Hare takes up a position which must be shared by Wittgenstein and his followers. They and Hare may differ in their positive views and in their emphasis, but they are alike in what they deny and alike in having to face the unpalatable consequences of that denial.

In his discussion of 'decisions of principle' Hare says:

If pressed to justify a decision completely, we have to give a complete specification of the way of life of which it is a part . . . If the inquirer still goes on asking 'But why *should* I live like that?' then there is no further answer to give him, because we have already *ex hypothesi* said everything that could be included in this further answer. We can only ask him to make up his own mind which way he ought to live: for in the end everything rests upon such a decision of principle. He has to decide whether to accept that way of life or not: if he accepts it, then we can proceed to justify the decisions that are based upon it; if he does not accept it, then let him accept some other, and try to live by it.[1]

Hare thinks that ultimately one can only commit oneself to a way of life, or reject it. The decision must be personal, and cannot be said to be right or wrong. All that is required is that I be willing to prescribe universally any principle I accept. Hare thus does at least stipulate a formal requirement for the making of moral commitments, and subordinates them to the demands of logic. However, he thinks that I cannot criticise those who profoundly disagree with me, any more than they can criticise me. I cannot therefore offer any argument against the views of 'fanatics' who are willing to prescribe universally their extreme views. Hare does not go as far as Wittgenstein and say that ethical views might be unintelligible to those who do not share them, but on Hare's own admission we are left in the uncomfortable position of being unable to say that, for instance, the Nazis' persecution of Jews was just morally *wrong*. Indeed, it is even unclear why, on his premises, Hare should dub the holders of such a view 'fanatics' (as he does). The mere fact that he does not hold a view should not give him the right to use any derogatory epithets about it, unless he is willing to accept that it is

[1] Hare, *The Language of Morals*, p. 69.

possible in principle to decide on a rational basis between competing moral commitments. This, however, is precisely what he is denying. As a result, there could be no criterion which we could use to discriminate between reasonable and unreasonable moral positions. Hare's use of the word 'fanaticism' about certain moral commitments shows how profoundly unsatisfactory his theory is. The concept of fanaticism, like that of superstition, presupposes the existence of objective standards to which we can appeal.

4

Forms of life

The importance of agreement

We have already noticed the argument that no justification of commitments is possible outside the way of life of which they form a part. In other words, no justification can be given for ways of life as such. We commit ourselves to one rather than another and that is all. As Wittgenstein says, 'What has to be accepted, the given, is – so one could say – *forms of life*.'[1]

We have seen how Wittgenstein insisted that there must be a certain agreement in judgments before people could share a concept. He emphasised that if, for instance, they did not generally agree in the judgments of colour, it could be impossible to say that they meant the same thing by such words as 'red' or 'blue'. He imagines a society where there was considerable disagreement, with one man saying a flower was red, while another called it blue. He asks: 'But what right should we have to call these people's words 'red' and 'blue' *our* colour-words. How would they learn to use these words?'[2] Agreement about the meaning of a word must, according to Wittgenstein, involve a general agreement about correct and incorrect uses of the word. When such agreement exists, the people share the same language, and, Wittgenstein says, 'to imagine a language means to imagine a form of life'. Without such agreement communication becomes impossible. The meaning of the words cannot then ever be taught in the first place.

It appears that a 'form of life' is a community of those sharing the same concepts. Basic conceptual disagreement

[1] Wittgenstein, *Philosophical Investigations*, p. 226.
[2] *Ibid.* § 19.

demonstrates a difference in 'forms of life'. This is somewhat imprecise and vague. How exactly can a 'form of life' be identified? Philosophers who have been influenced by the notion have understood it in different ways. One of the most obvious places where it might seem relevant is where two distinct social systems are compared. For example, S. E. Toulmin deals with the problem of justification in ethics, and follows the line that social practices must be understood in terms of the ways of life of which they are part. He maintains:

All that can be compared are the ways of life *as wholes*, and *this* comparison is, if anything, a private one . . . reason as one may, the final decision is personal. There is no magic word which will turn the English social system into a Muslim one overnight: the only practical use for the question, 'Which way of life is the better?' is in the service of a personal decision – for example whether to remain here in our society, such as it is, or to go and live as an Arab tribesman in the desert.[1]

Toulmin complicates the matter by also referring to the 'Christian way of life', which obviously can exist in different social systems. His emphasis on the ultimate nature of a commitment to a way of life makes it all the more crucial that it should be clear what exactly counts as a way of life. Similar confusion occurs when philosophers are dealing specifically with Wittgenstein's concept of a form of life. D. M. High sets out to talk of what he calls the 'human form of life of Western culture' but maintains that animal life is a form of life and different from that of human life.[2] He considers that this is the basis of Wittgenstein's remark that if a lion could talk, we could not understand him.[3] Even if High is right about this, the lions' form of life would presumably be different from those of other animals, so that animal life as such could not be a 'form of life'. When one compares this

[1] Toulmin, *The Place of Reason in Ethics*, p. 153.
[2] High, *Language, Persons and Beliefs*, p. 100.
[3] Wittgenstein, *Philosophical Investigations*, p. 223.

with Winch's view[1] that science is one mode of social life, and religion is another, it becomes clear that the concept of a form of life is capable of many interpretations. One common theme is the self-contained nature of forms of life. It is usually stressed that they have their own criterion of intelligibility, and cannot be fully understood from the outside. To dub something a 'form of life' is in effect to protect it from criticism.

A clear danger which can result from this approach is that all serious disagreements in religion, ethics and any other field could be explained as arising from different forms of life. Once it is thought that any moral outlook is rooted in a form of life, and that a fundamental difference in moral outlook must be explained by a difference in forms of life, it could become a matter of definition that whenever there was a basic disagreement, a difference in forms of life could be found. In this way, the concept could be made trivial and uninteresting. To invoke it would merely show determination not to admit the possibility that the disagreement was in principle soluble, or that either or both parties in the dispute were wrong. Unless there is some independent criterion for identifying forms of life apart from moral disagreement, the concept is useless in explaining the disagreement. It is unimpressive to be told that a certain moral disagreement can only be explained by the difference in forms of life from which those in disagreement come, and then to find that the disagreement is itself the only criterion for identifying the two forms of life.

Forms of life in morality

R. W. Beardsmore applies Wittgenstein's conception of a form of life to ethics and maintains: 'What does and what does not count as a moral consideration is determined by the

[1] Winch, *The Idea of a Social Science*, p. 100.

way of life to which an individual belongs.'[1] A man must first commit himself to a way of life before he can be understood to be making any moral judgment. Reasons for action can only be seen to be such if they are grounded in a particular system of morality. It follows that a reason for one man may not be a reason for another, if they owe allegiance to different moralities. Beardsmore specifically presses this point to explain moral disagreement. He accepts Wittgenstein's point that there must be an agreement in judgments as a precondition for the sharing of concepts, and claims that this agreement is to be found *within* a particular moral code. He maintains that it may be impossible to settle a disagreement between moral codes. In fact he should go further than he does, if he wishes to follow Wittgenstein's thinking through to its logical conclusion. He should maintain not just that certain moral disagreements arising between different moralities are insoluble, but that such cases are instances of mutual moral incomprehension rather than mere disagreement. If agreement is a precondition for language, it follows that those who basically and persistently disagree are in effect using a different language. They have different concepts. This is, of course, a very implausible analysis of moral disagreement. To take an example used by Beardsmore[2] it is certainly controversial whether vivisection is morally justified as a part of scientific method. There is disagreement over whether the suffering caused to animals is an overriding consideration against vivisection. Does it outweigh the advantages for research of experiments on live animals? Both the scientist and the anti-vivisectionist understand what the other is saying. They probably both agree that the infliction of suffering is a bad thing. The disagreement is over the weight to be given this. The views of each are completely intelligible to the other.

[1] Beardsmore, *Moral Reasoning*, p. 130.
[2] *Ibid.* pp. 106ff.

Beardsmore does not talk of mutual incomprehension in this kind of case. Instead he merely emphasises the different importance given to the same fact. He also thinks it impossible to criticise either way of life. As a result the disagreement must remain. He says:

When these ways of life come into conflict, there is no neutral standard, no 'common evidence' by which the dispute can be resolved. The standards of relevance are themselves in dispute. Because of this, it does not make sense to say that there must be a solution to the dispute.[1]

We shall postpone a full discussion of religious and moral disagreement till later. The point to be emphasised here is Beardsmore's glib assumption that the disagreement between the scientist and the anti-vivisectionist can be explained by talking of 'ways of life'. He says:

In order to account for the dispute, we have to realise that the scientist has been brought up in an environment where great importance is attached to the scientific way of life. The anti-vivisectionist by contrast has been influenced by his contact with those who oppose suffering, but who do not necessarily attach any overriding importance to the aims and purposes of scientists.[2]

Beardsmore's sole reason for making these large assertions is that the scientist and anti-vivisectionist disagree about the relative importance of animal suffering. This in fact seems to constitute the difference between the two 'ways of life'. Beardsmore does not consider the position of a dedicated scientist who opposes vivisection. The distinction between the two 'ways of life' seems to break down at this point. They are clearly not necessarily as self-contained as he assumes. It would be difficult to separate them out from society. In fact the very idea of an anti-vivisectionist way of life seems highly unconvincing. As a method of explaining moral disagreement the notion of separate self-contained ways of life may be of use if they are really separate and self-

[1] Beardsmore, *Moral Responsibility*, p. 108.
[2] *Ibid.*

contained. If they do not have any existence except as the sources of the disagreement, the notion loses all explanatory power. It is worth noting, too, the kind of explanation they would provide. As Beardsmore describes the situation, the disagreement between the scientist and the anti-vivisectionist is to be explained by the different upbringings each received. In other words, it appears to be some kind of causal explanation, and it certainly may show why those individuals think as they do. It does nothing to show why one of them cannot be right and the other wrong. The mere fact that one of them will not accept as an overriding reason what the other does accept becomes less significant if we can blame their upbringing for their obstinacy.

If Beardsmore wishes to maintain the stronger thesis that their moral concepts are rooted in their way of life it is very strange that they seem perfectly able to understand the other's point of view. They know what they are rejecting. This suggests that in fact they share the same moral concepts. They know what they mean by evil, and may even agree about many of the things they call evil. They merely disagree as to how evil animal suffering is.

Perhaps it may be felt that Beardsmore picked an unfortunate example. Two other philosophers have also faced the problem of the deadlock which occurs in ethics when two people agree on all the facts, but still disagree about what ought to be done.[1] They give the examples of a Roman Catholic housewife arguing with a scientific rationalist about birth control, and a pacifist arguing with a militarist. They go on to say: 'The rationalist, the housewife, the pacifist, or the militarist cannot say what they like. Their arguments are rooted in different moral traditions within which there are rules for what can and cannot be said.' Different things would be important for each tradition, and it would be impossible to provide any standards with which

[1] D. Z. Phillips and H. O. Mounce, in *Philosophy* XL (1965), 317–18.

to decide between the traditions. Moral standards, in other words, must stem from a prior commitment. Moral concepts get a grip *within* a tradition and have no existence outside. The concept of a moral tradition in fact owes a great deal to that of a form of life. It is equally vague, and depends on an unrealistic view of moral traditions as separate and self-contained. The pacifist moral tradition only exists in so far as there is a disagreement on the pacifist issue. The pacifist could be on either side in the argument between the housewife and the rationalist. To explain the disagreement between pacifist and militarist in terms of moral traditions is to do more than emphasise the existence of the disagreement. To posit different moral traditions for every fundamental moral disagreement is to reduce to absurdity the notion of a form of life, a way of life, or a moral tradition. It is to engender an indefinite number of forms of life. For example, we would no doubt have to distinguish the anti-vivisectionist pacifist from the anti-vivisectionist non-pacifist, and so on, with ever more complicated moral traditions to explain complicated moral outlooks. If it is to be accepted that fundamental moral disagreement indicates that each person in the dispute has a different conceptual framework, it will become necessary to start subdividing what are apparently promising candidates for forms of life. For instance, the Roman Catholic Church does provide an example of an apparently unified moral tradition with traditional emphases. It might seem plausible to suppose that it does have rules which govern what can and cannot be correctly said within the tradition, and that as a result something like birth control is seen as simply wrong. Because the Roman Church can be clearly identified apart from its disagreements over such issues with non-Catholics, to say that it provides a separate form of life is not trivial. Yet disagreements as fundamental as any which occur between Catholic and non-Catholic rage between Catholics over moral questions. Despite Rome's traditional opposition to many methods of birth control, many otherwise loyal Catholics seriously question or actually condemn the traditional attitude. Are we therefore to say that within the Roman Church there is a pro-birth-control form of life, and an anti-birth-control one?

Certainly those putting forward the 'forms of life' view would accept that where there is an agreement in language, particular disagreement on specific occasions is possible within the common conceptual framework. We are not here saying that on their view each moral disagreement *must* entail a different conceptual system. We are pointing out that in the absence of clear criteria for identifying forms of life, the existence of seemingly insoluble disagreement within an apparent form of life could well be a sign that we are here dealing with two forms of life. We have as much reason for saying this as for saying that there is a disagreement within one form of life, and we have no sensible way of deciding what to say.

Beardsmore deals with an analogous problem when he maintains that within Catholic morality the question 'Is suicide wrong?' is redundant.[1] If the question arises for a particular Catholic, he says, the considerations which give sense to the question are not Catholic considerations. 'The doubt,' he maintains, 'comes from outside the Catholic morality.' Presumably in the birth-control case he would also wish to say that Catholics supporting birth control are being swayed by non-Catholic considerations. In other words, in so far as Catholics even question features of traditional Catholic morality they are much less committed to Catholicism. According to this view, membership of a particular morality involves blind obedience to the traditional standard of that morality. Once it is admitted that members of one morality can be influenced by the

[1] Beardsmore, *Moral Reasoning*, pp. 102–3.

considerations that are given importance in another morality, the notion of self-contained forms of life collapses. It could perhaps be accepted that different forms of life overlap. Winch gives the example of someone having religious reasons for devoting his life to science. This, however, is very different from the situation where there are two competing forms of life, such as two moralities. To suggest that a person belonging to one would not merely find the other intelligible but even be influenced by it is to empty of all meaning the concept of a form of life. Instead one could merely start talking of competing moral views. The only force the doctrine about forms of life might still have is that in the last resort one cannot justify the adoption of one moral position rather than another. This is merely the kind of position adopted by R. M. Hare, and is very far from Wittgenstein's idea of forms of life, which was linked with his explanation of the nature of concepts.

Neither Wittgenstein nor any of those influenced by him have given any clear indication of how a form of life is to be identified. It might perhaps be enlightening if applied to the study of geographically separate societies in some such field as social anthropology. It can only be confusing if applied to the areas of contemporary religion and morality in order to explain the fundamental disagreements which undoubtedly exist. We only have to ask whether religion, Christianity or a particular Christian denomination such as Catholicism should be regarded as a form of life. There is no clear way of answering such a question, and it is significant that we have found each one accepted as a form of life by some philosopher.

The 'distinctiveness' of religious language

Any philosopher who wishes to protect from criticism religion in general or any particular religion may try to fence it off by saying that religious language is separate from other language and has a logic of its own. To attribute such a motive is clearly not a substitute for philosophical argument, but it may certainly sometimes explain why philosophers are led to positions which have puzzling consequences. Tillich, for instance, claims: 'The religious language, the language of symbol and myth, is created in the community of believers and cannot be fully understood outside the community.'[1] Many philosophers emphasise the logical necessity for the participation of a religious believer in a shared language. He must learn religious language and it is stressed that this is a special kind of language. D. Z. Phillips goes so far as to suggest that to know how to use this language *is* to know God.[2] As a result, only the committed could be able to use the language. It would then be impossible for agnostics or atheists to take part in any discussion about religion because by definition they would have no grasp of religious concepts.

This kind of view is often linked with the equally obscure idea that religion is a form of life. If religious language is the language of the religious form of life, it is clearly important either to be able to identify the religious form of life or alternatively to mark off religious language from other types. It is significant that writers from a Christian background use 'religion' to mean the Christian religion. Talk of God (even the Christian God) is not confined to the Christian Church, and the thesis that religious language is a special form of language with its own rules becomes much more questionable if it is made clear that what is meant is *Christian* language. Indeed, if this is interpreted strictly to mean the language used by *committed* Christians (those who *agree* in their judgments) a very great deal of talk of God, much of it reverent and within the scope of the Christian tradition, is thereby

[1] Tillich, *Dynamics of Faith*, p. 24.
[2] Phillips, *The Concept of Prayer*, p. 50.

excluded. Even if one accepted a wider definition of Christian language so that it could be accepted that even those who were uncommitted could use it, there is clearly a large area of religious language still excluded. It is only necessary to think of the many other religions which exist alongside Christianity. Sometimes, it is true, two religions may be so radically different that the claims of one are almost unintelligible to those committed to the other, but it seems very rash to say *a priori* that this must be so. It ought merely to be possible to accept that the members of different religions might understand each other and disagree. There seems to be no *a priori* reason why Christian language should be fundamentally different from other types of religious language.

Talk of God has been mentioned as a central case of religious language but this raises a further problem. Should religious language be thought restricted to statements about God? Clearly this would be to restrict the use of the term far too much. It rules out *a priori* the very possibility of an atheistic religion. Yet once its scope is widened, the view that religious language is a special kind of language, totally distinct from the language we use in non-religious contexts, becomes less persuasive. It is easy to make distinctions between talk of God and talk of material objects (no doubt because God, if He exists, is not a material object). As a result, religious language can be made to appear very special and mysterious. When, however, it is recognised that religious language has a place in a wider context, its use is linked by many to religious commitment in a very intimate fashion. But once our distinction between the two elements essential for any commitment is introduced, it becomes clear that the acceptance of certain propositions can be logically separated from the personal response which would normally follow. Religious language cannot then be identified by the place it is given in a person's life. The important thing about talk of God is that it is about God. The place it holds in the life of an individual must be a secondary consideration.

Talk about God in particular and religious language in general should not be linked too closely with the lives of those who indulge in it. Otherwise one is involved in a circularity. We would have to understand what statements about God mean by the difference they make to the lives of individuals and we would have to explain that difference in terms of their belief in God. Thus their belief in God must be understood in terms of their own way of life and their way of life in terms of their belief in God. This is only saved from vicious circularity if it is agreed that ways of life must be accepted and not explained. In fact, however, to say that someone acts in a certain way because of his belief in God does seem to be more than a redescription of his action. It is not just to place it in its context. It is to give a *reason* for it. The belief is distinct from the commitment which may follow it, and is the justification for it.

All this is not to deny that there is some connection between belief and action. The concept of hypocrisy clearly depends on the view that there is one, but beliefs are not so linked with actions that they can only be understood in terms of them. The point is that if certain things are believed to be true, it is rational to act in a certain way. If someone comes to believe that there is a God, who created men and cares for them, we would expect his life to be influenced by the belief. In so far as he refuses to allow it to affect his attitude to other people and still, for example, maintains that there is no reason why he should bother about other people's troubles, he is being irrational. In such a case the temptation would always be for the observer to say that the man's belief was not genuine and that he was a hypocrite. We have already seen that this would be to simplify the situation unduly. In fact, religious beliefs are not very different from other beliefs as far as their relation to action is concerned. The main difference lies in their subject matter. Religious beliefs are concerned with what is regarded as being of ultimate importance. As a result, they inevitably have a profound influence which permeates the whole of a man's life. It is for this reason that we expect religion to make a difference to someone in a way in which everyday factual beliefs clearly will not. To revert to the example we used at the beginning of chapter 2, my belief that there are elephants in Africa is hardly likely to influence my behaviour if I am not interested in elephants. My beliefs about the purpose and meaning of life, on the other hand, should clearly have a very great influence. They do not depend on my interests, but rather determine to a large extent what my interests will be.

It follows from all this that religious language is unlikely to be totally distinct from other kinds of discourse. If religious belief has affinities with non-religious belief, it would be surprising if the language expressing that belief was of a logically different type from the language expressing other kinds of belief. Certainly any view which emphasises the distinct and peculiar nature of religious language is bound to provide some kind of criterion to enable us to identify religious language in the first place. If it can easily be distinguished from other types of language, it ought to be possible to specify its special characteristics.

Whether language is being used in a religious way or not often seems to depend on the context. The exclamation 'Oh, God!' could be an agonised prayer from the heart, or a trivial blasphemy. Philosophers talking about proofs for the existence of God may in a sense be talking about God, but it seems odd to say that they are using religious language. If not every reference to God can necessarily be classified as 'religious', it may be that the notion of religious language is after all linked closely with that of religious commitment.

Religious language would be understood as the language used in connection with a particular religion by those committed to it. So far from it being a distinctive brand of language it would be language used in a particular context. The same language used in a different situation by someone who had no religious commitment would not be religious; for example by someone denying the claims of a particular religion. Such a person should be distinguished from the man who dismisses everything said in connection with religion as meaningless. The latter is not denying the truth of any religious claims. He is denying that any claims are being made. This is a more sophisticated approach and usually means that some philosophical axe is being ground. The person who denies religious claims, however, understands them and rejects them. In his denial he is using precisely the same form of words as the religious believer, with the addition of the negative. It would seem impossible to suggest that the difference between 'Jesus rose from the dead' and 'Jesus did not rise from the dead' is that we have moved from one kind of language to another. It is surely more reasonable to assume that in each case the same kind of language is being used. The negation of a sentence does not alter the sense of the sentence in any other way. Indeed the whole point of the negation is that what is being negated *does* retain precisely the same sense as when it is asserted. Otherwise atheists and theists would necessarily be talking about different things.

If religious language is not a special kind of language, insulated from ordinary language, but is merely the language especially used by those who have a religious commitment, it is not surprising that some philosophers have tried to make too close a link between the language and the commitment. This has had the result once again of marking off religious language from other types of language. Indeed, if the language is thought of as an expression of the commitment, the fact of commitment becomes part of the meaning of religious language. I. T. Ramsey provides an example of this approach. He stresses that religious language is, in his phrase 'logically odd' and very different from 'straightforward' language. For instance, he contrasts the question 'Did the Resurrection occur?' with the question 'Did Queen Anne's occur?' He continues:

If the word 'Resurrection' refers to such 'data' as an 'empty tomb', visions, etc., all these might not only have happened but be believed without in any sense there being a Christian belief in the Resurrection; without there being Christian commitment. It might, for instance, always be said that there was an earthquake; that parallels could be drawn from abnormal psychology, and so on. So, 'Did the Resurrection occur?' has *not* the same logic as 'Did the empty tomb occur?'[1]

Ramsey says in justification of the last statement that the fact of the empty tomb can be accepted while the Resurrection is denied and *vice versa*. Clearly the Resurrection involves a more complex set of beliefs than merely a belief that the tomb was found to be empty (a fact for which there could certainly be more than one explanation). This of itself does not show that the Resurrection is something which is in a different logical category from ordinary historical events. Ramsey also maintains that it is possible to assert the truth of the Resurrection and deny the fact of the empty tomb. This seems highly dubious from the standpoint of orthodox Christian belief, but the interesting point is his tendency to empty religious beliefs of their factual content and to emphasise the importance of commitment instead. He admits that evidence is relevant, but insists that no amount of evidence could guarantee the Resurrection, which must go beyond all empirical criteria, and break the bounds of the merely spatio-temporal. Ramsey places far too much emphasis on the reaction of the individual to certain situations, and too little on the objective features of the situations. As a result, for him

[1] Ramsey, *Religious Language*, p. 127.

the Resurrection seems to refer as much to a person's reaction to what took place as to the event itself. He expressly distinguishes the Resurrection from the empty tomb and denies that the former can be dated. He says moreover, that it is, strictly speaking, impossible to be doubtful about the Resurrection. Either one believes it or one is converted to 'infidelity'. There is no middle way. He claims: 'The truth of the Resurrection is logically integrated with our full commitment in Christ.'[1] It is clear that he must think that the very meaning of the term 'Resurrection' is also integrated with our commitment. He considers that it is something which cannot be identified or even talked of without the existence of the religious commitment which invests certain events with significance.

The Resurrection has always held a central place in the Christian faith, and belief in it has always been thought to be a major reason for Christian commitment. It was the Resurrection which the early Christians preached. St Paul epitomises the orthodox Christian view when he says: 'If Christ be not raised, your faith is vain.'[2] If it is believed that Christ did rise from the dead, this must have a major effect on the believer's attitude to Him. It is important to stress that as a matter of logic (if not in fact) commitment *follows* belief in the Resurrection. People do not believe the truth of the Resurrection because they are committed to Christ. It must be the other way round. They follow Christ because they believe in the Resurrection (amongst other things). Any connection between beliefs and commitment is of the same kind in religion as in any other sphere of life. The belief provides a reason for commitment, but is logically separate from it. The belief could occur without the commitment, even where what is believed in is the Resurrection. It may be irrational, but it is not impossible for someone to accept the

[1] Ramsey, *Religious Language*, p. 131.
[2] 1 Corinthians 15:17.

truth of the Christian gospel, Resurrection and all, and still refuse to base his life on it.

Ramsey's view of commitment as being an 'all or nothing' affair, with a stark choice between 'infidelity' and 'full commitment' is reminiscent of Wittgenstein's treatment of religious beliefs. It is no accident that for both Ramsey[1] and Wittgenstein there is no room for doubt in religious belief, since in their eyes doubt must be a weakening of commitment. Their position follows naturally from their playing down of the propositional element in religious belief and from this emphasis on commitment, with the result that the propositional element becomes regarded as part of the commitment instead of providing the grounds and reasons for it. Ramsey's acceptance of the possibility of someone with a religious commitment and a belief in the Resurrection denying that the tomb was empty suggests that he is willing to go so far as to give up the whole notion of propositional belief in religious commitment. However, merely because in Christian belief the Resurrection is something more than a matter of an empty tomb, it does not follow that the Resurrection can be accepted apart from the empty tomb. It was certainly more than that, but it was at least that according to Christian doctrine.

Ramsey's emphasis of the logical peculiarity of religious utterances leads in only one direction, that of claiming religious language to be totally separate from other language. To say that religious language is logically odd is to begin to tread a path which inevitably leads to the placing of religious beliefs beyond the scope of reason and evidence. Ramsey himself is unwilling to give up the idea that evidence *is* relevant for belief in the Resurrection, but the line of his argument seems to be against his own feelings in the matter.

It is clearly a gross simplification to treat religious language

[1] Ramsey, *Religious Language*, p. 130.

as a homogeneous whole. Our purpose here is not to discuss the nature of religious language as such, but to stress that its use does not depend on a prior religious commitment, as it would if religion was a form of life. Neither does the meaning of religious language as such include the notion of religious commitment. To talk of the 'Resurrection' is to talk of an event which may or may not have occurred. It is not to talk of anyone's beliefs about the significance of that event.

If religious language is the language used in connection with their beliefs by those who have adopted a religious commitment, it will clearly be very far from being of one type. It will include poetic language, language which attempts to express the inexpressible, technical theological language, statements about history and so on. Religious language is not totally distinct from language used in other contexts, nor is it in itself of a uniform type. It is not a separate kind of language at all.

The position of the unbeliever

The idea that religious language is totally distinct from other types of language often receives support from the difficulty of believers in communicating their faith to non-believers. This kind of empirical consideration, however, is irrelevant to any conceptual question. The fact that many do not seem to make any sense of religious claims does not of itself show that the claims have no sense. The claims of Christianity are the same this year as they were in times when they met with more ready acceptance. It would be ridiculous to suppose that their meaning fluctuated according to the response they evoked. The dangers of linking too closely the fact of commitment and the problem of meaning are readily apparent. If few people now become committed to a particular religion, it might seem to follow that the claims of that religion had become meaningless, at least for the majority. The meaningfulness of certain statements might then seem to be a matter of counting heads. There is a distinction between finding something meaningless in the sense of seeing no point in it, and finding it meaningless in the sense of not understanding it. The fact that many find religion 'meaningless' does not by itself entail that religious statements have no meaning. Much the same could be said of 'unintelligible'. To talk of the unintelligibility of religion to modern man may be saying more about modern man than about religion. It is to talk of what he cannot understand, and here too there may be a slide from one sense of 'understand' to another. Someone may not understand why another person gets so caught up in some great political cause. He cannot see the sense of bothering about it, although he is quite aware of what the political cause is. This is totally different from the same person's inability to understand, say, Russian. In the same way it is important to distinguish between a failure to understand religion in the sense of not seeing the point of it, and a failure to understand what is being said by religious people in the way one does not understand some foreign language (or worse in the way in which one does not understand talk of 'slythy toves gyring and gimbling').

Many contemporary writers on the philosophy of religion do not make these distinctions. A failure to differentiate between propositional belief and the commitment which is the normal response to it provides one reason for the confusion. If I, in one sense, understood religious claims but failed to see their importance, I should remain as much uncommitted to any religion as if the claims seemed so much gibberish. A failure to understand in either sense has the same result. If all our attention is diverted to the fact of commitment and none to the importance of certain beliefs, it becomes unimportant why someone rejects Christianity.

He is uncommitted, and that is all that matters. One can ask, however, whether the man understood the claims of Christianity and rejected them because he thought them false, found them nonsensical or couched in unintelligible language, or whether he just did not see their relevance or importance. In the last case, he understands the claims, and his difficulty lies with the need to commit himself, while in the former cases he is more concerned with the claims of Christianity as such.

The position of unbelievers will not be completely explained by any one analysis. There are different ways of finding religious claims meaningless, and there are many who would wish to dismiss them as being false. It is a gross simplification to suggest that non-believers react in any uniform way to religion. Yet S. C. Brown – in dealing with the whole question of the meaning of religious claims – starts from the basic assumption that the unbeliever is not able to attach sense to the claims of religion and considers that his main task is to give a single explanation for the existence of this 'intelligibility gap' as he calls it. He accepts that the gap may only be apparent, on the grounds that religious claims may lack meaning even for those who put them forward. He nowhere considers the possibility that at least some un-believers may find religious claims perfectly intelligible, and *for that reason* find them false. He refuses to accept that they could know what it would be for religious beliefs to be true, and baldly says: 'On the face of it, the religious believer seems to be committed to claims which he (presumably) finds intelligible. Yet these claims are not found intelligible by the non-believer.'[1]

Brown concludes that although there are connections between religious language and everyday language, the norms of intelligibility which govern discourse in a particular religion are to be found implicit in that discourse. We are

[1] Brown, *Do Religious Claims Make Sense?* p. 137.

back with the view that commitment to a religion and understanding of it go hand in hand. Included in the notion of entering such a commitment is the idea of a conceptual change. It follows that no-one who is uncommitted can understand religious claims, presumably in the sense of 'understand' in which one does not understand a foreign language. After starting with what seemed to be an empirical generalisation about the attitude of unbelievers to religion today, Brown has arrived at a position somewhat similar to that of Wittgenstein, and has laid down *a priori* what the reaction of the unbeliever *must* be to religion. Clearly, however, the empirical question must be kept distinct from the conceptual one.

It is rash to say that the unbeliever logically cannot understand the claims of religion, but it is equally rash to suppose that he must. Many religious statements are uttered against a background of belief, and anyone who does not share the presuppositions of the speaker may find it difficult to understand what is being said. Talk of the 'Son of God' may not be very enlightening to someone who will not accept that there is a God. Much that is said in a religious context may be unintelligible to non-believers without some explanation of what is being presupposed and without some elucidation of technical terms. In the same way the language of scientists may be almost completely unintelligible to non-scientists without lengthy explanation. This is one reason why the language of faith seems different from that of the philosophical examination of religion. In the former many things are taken for granted, while it is the job of the latter to examine all presuppositions. It remains, however, a contingent matter how much is presupposed and how many technical terms are employed by the man of faith. The words he uses to describe his faith to other believers may be very different from those which he uses in talking to an atheist. A bald reference to the 'Grace of God' would be adequate on the first occasion, but would probably only mystify on the second. Yet he may be saying basically the same thing on both occasions. There can be no clear distinction between the two of the kind which C. B. Martin wishes to make. He differentiates between statements 'in the faith' and statements 'outside the faith'. He maintains that the former are ritualistic and are thought to rely on the authority of God. Unlike the latter, they are secure from external challenge. He says:

The problem of how the Christian story can be said to be true or false may engage us, though not the man in the faith. This does not mean the same man cannot make statements both inside and outside the faith. It means that statements made in the faith have a certain security. So long as a man remains in the faith, he has sanctuary from the probings of philosophical debate.[1]

There is a difference between merely expressing one's beliefs and attempting to justify them. The language of faith presupposes more than does the language of philosophy. Martin, however, thinks that there are 'two different ways of speaking in religious language' and this makes it look as if he is saying that religious language can be divided into two logical categories, in only one of which the question of truth or falsity arises. Statements made 'in the faith' are protected from criticism. This seems a very curious view. Martin clearly has in mind the fact that what may count as a reason for someone within the faith may not do so for someone outside. That something has the authority of God behind it is a powerful reason for the theist and no reason at all for the atheist. Yet at the same time, Martin wants to allow argument about religious beliefs and it remains unclear how statements in the faith can be protected if any challenge to the faith itself is successful. He does not consider the precise relationship between the two ways of speaking in religious language, but they cannot be totally unrelated. If there was

[1] Martin, *Religious Belief*, p. 134.

no connection between them, a man speaking outside the faith could become convinced of the falsity of his religion, and still speak in the faith. In fact if he did so, he would be involved in very grave inconsistency. If it is accepted that religious faith can be true or false, the very possibility of speaking sincerely in the faith depends on a belief in the truth of the faith. As a result, any distinction between statements in the faith and statements outside the faith cannot be made merely on the pretext that the former is outside the domain of truth and falsity. Martin's distinction can be reduced to the trivial observation that assuming the truth of what one is speaking about, or expressing a belief in it, is different from questioning its truth.

Statements made 'in the faith' are in fact statements made in a certain context, against a certain background. They are not statements with an idiosyncratic logic. Once their context is appreciated there is no bar to those outside the faith understanding the statements, and denying their truth.

Religion and truth

Relativists often like to talk of 'different worlds' and D. Z. Phillips, for example, says that it is wrong to think of religion and humanism as competing interpretations of the same constant 'phenomena'. He continues: 'Religious language is not an interpretation of how things are, but determines how things are for the believer. The saint and the atheist do not interpret the same world in different ways. They see different worlds.'[1] Full communication between them must be then ruled out, and in fact Phillips holds that the atheist has to be someone who cannot make any sense of what is rejected.[2] He does not allow that religion can make any claims to truth. Rational rejection of religion is impossible. He says

[1] Phillips, *Faith and Philosophical Enquiry*, p. 132.
[2] Phillips (ed.), *Religion and Understanding*, p. 79.

quite explicitly that 'the man who has no use for the religious picture is not contradicting the believer'.[1]

One consequence of the insistence that religious concepts, like other kinds of concept, càn only be understood in the context from which they derive their meaning, is that an 'all-embracing' view of truth has to be rejected. One cannot step outside every form of life and then decide what is true. Criteria for truth are on this view rooted in the life of which they are part, and even different religions may have different criteria. This makes it easier for Phillips to hold that a wrong view of truth is being imposed on Christianity, when it is supposed that Christianity is making factual claims. He says: 'One might object to my analysis on the grounds that it stresses religious meaning at the expense of religious truth. The analysis does not indicate which religion is the true one. But why should anyone suppose that philosophy can answer that question?'[2]

It is no function of the philosophy of religion to advocate a particular religion as being true. To object, however, that Phillips is emphasising meaning at the expense of truth is not to ask him to preach Christianity. It is to point out that although he may be able to say what talk of truth *within* a particular religion amounts to, he has removed the possibility of saying that Christianity, or any other religion, as a whole is true or false. The philosopher (*qua* philosopher) cannot be concerned with whether Christianity is true, but whether it is the kind of thing which can be true clearly is a philosophical question. Phillips' failure to realise this stems from his belief that it is impossible to talk of an independent reality against which religions can be measured. He ignores the fact that many people do wish to talk of religions as such being true or false.

Phillips would deny that he is ignoring truth in connection

[1] Phillips, *Death and Immortality*, p. 76.
[2] Phillips, *Faith and Philosophical Enquiry*, p. 11.

with religion, although he regards it as a strength of his position that it rules out the possibility of any external justification of religion. He follows Wittgenstein in talking of the strength of the 'picture' in religious belief, but sees the difficulties which arise as a result of his insistence that apart from the 'pictures' of religious believers there is no way of conceiving of God. He says:

Wittgenstein stressed in his lectures that the whole weight may be in the picture. The picture is not a picturesque way of saying something else. It says what it says, and when the picture dies, something dies with it, and there can be no substitute for that which dies with the picture.[1]

The question Phillips then faces is what happens if the pictures die and people no longer live a religious life. Are we to suppose that God dies? The mere fact that he can consider this question as a possible consequence of the death of the picture shows how closely he links God with the pictures of Him current in a religious form of life. He is unable to think of God existing apart from our thought of Him, and elsewhere considers the objection that he is denying the objective reality of God. He suggests three possible interpretations of the objection, the first being that the believer creates his belief. Phillips points out that a religious believer does not create a tradition but is born into one. 'He cannot,' we are told, 'say whatever he likes about God, since there are criteria which determine what it makes sense to say.'[2] These criteria are, of course, those of the form of life, and we might well wonder here whether Phillips has not jumped out of the frying pan of subjectivism into the fire of relativism. The second thing he considers an objector might mean is that it is impossible to be mistaken about the nature of God, and Phillips does allow some place for mistake within religion. Thirdly, he recognises that the objector might be accusing him of saying that God is not an object. Phillips demon-

[1] Phillips, *Faith and Philosophical Enquiry*, p. 119.
[2] *Ibid.* p. 59.

strates that God cannot be a thing, since if He were He would be finite. The most interesting point in all this is that he does not consider the most natural interpretation of the objection, which is that the existence of God is in no way dependent on our individual or collective thought of Him. This is an indispensable part of the concept of the Christian God. Part at least of the notion of God as Creator must involve the belief that God existed when men did not. It is obvious, too, that the very idea of God being limited by being dependent on anything or anybody must be incoherent.

Phillips' answer to the question of the possible death of God is somewhat tentative but he thinks 'that the desire to say that God dies is literal-mindedness attempting to reassert itself'.[1] In other words, the desire is merely motivated by a conception of a God existing apart from the picture. Phillips wants to go much further than merely saying that the existence of God is dependent on our thought of Him. He wants to link God so closely with the pictures influencing the life of the believer that it becomes impossible to conceive of God as existing at all apart from the picture. Without any picture men may no longer wish to talk or think of God, and may indeed have no conception of God at all. This is part of what is meant by the picture dying and may amount to no more than the trivial truth that when men do not think or speak of God, they do not think or speak of God. It is, however, meaningful to suggest that God would exist even then, and this is what Phillips cannot say. It is no contradiction to think of a time when no-one acknowledged God. Phillips in fact would agree with this. He says: 'Religious believers can say something now, from within the picture, about such a time of radical absence of belief. What they say is not that God has died, but that in such a time, people have turned their backs on God.'[2]

[1] Phillips, *Faith and Philosophical Enquiry*, p. 120.
[2] Phillips, *Death and Immortality*, p. 78.

However, he points out that when anyone talks of such a time, they are speaking now when conceptions of God are still alive. They are within the picture and 'there is nothing within belief which allows them to say that God can die'.[1] Their talk of people turning their backs on God is thus merely a consequence of the picture they hold, and has no implications concerning the existence of God in an age of unbelief. At such a time no-one would talk of God, and what believers say about such a time will merely be a reflection of their own belief. When this has been said, the most important question has still not been touched, namely, whether God could continue to exist even if no-one believed in Him. Are those who have lost all religious belief at fault in that they are ignoring what is true, and are present-day believers justified in their conception of a continuing God? The very picture which, according to Phillips, allows believers to talk of people turning their backs on God itself presupposes that God can exist when people ignore Him. Although he wants to avoid thinking of God as existing apart from the pictures which believers have, the pictures themselves demand that this happen.

Phillips' idiosyncratic views on truth appear when he faces the general point that 'there are no agreed public tests whereby true and false can be distinguished in religious claims'. He retorts: 'There are various criteria recognised by religious believers for what can and cannot be said to God and about God. It is not true that there are no tests for what is truly religious.'[2]

There is a slide in this from the truth and falsity of religious claims to what is 'truly religious'. Phillips seems to think that in talking about the latter, he is somehow answering the former. Given his refusal to accept the possibility of any external justification of religion, he can only allow for talk of

[1] Phillips, *Faith and Philosophical Enquiry*, p. 120.
[2] *Ibid.* p. 153.

truth *within* religion, and his emphasis on the criteria accepted by religious believers follows from this. There is then room for talk of true and false religion, but none for talk of a religion as such being true or false. It is no use pretending that any point about the truth and falsity of religious claims can be fully met by merely distinguishing between what is and is not truly religious. If religious claims are true, they are true whether people believe them or not, and they ought to be accepted by everyone. The mere establishment of something as 'truly religious' says nothing about whether anybody should be religious. There may be criteria for deciding what is truly Marxist, but there is no contradiction in agreeing that a certain viewpoint is truly Marxist and rejecting Marxism as such. The existence of criteria for what is 'truly Christian' still leaves open the question whether Christianity is true. Phillips may wish to rule out the possibility of Christianity as such being true or false, but any attempt to import talk of truth in religion in some other way must be highly confusing.

He is insistent that religion is 'not all a matter of personal decision or commitment'. In other words, we cannot ourselves decide what is to count as Christian. There are standards current in the religious community, and even if the idea of an all-embracing truth is removed, the result is not total anarchy. Phillips points out: 'If a man said that God had told him in a vision to eliminate all coloured people from the face of the earth, this would not be accepted by the Christian community as a vision from God.'[1]

Phillips will not allow us to ask whether the Christian community has a true view of God, or even whether they are right to think there is a God. We can agree that the man has had a vision which is very much at variance with Christianity. According to Phillips, however, we cannot go further and say that the man has a *wrong* conception of God, or, at

[1] *Idem.*

least, if we did, we would be doing nothing more than reiterating our own Christian commitment. As a result the idea of an ultimate, arbitrary commitment reappears, despite Phillips' efforts to dismiss it. We certainly cannot, if we are Christians, commit ourselves to any view we please, but we are perfectly free to decide not to be Christians. The existence of a Christian community puts no limitation at all on what view we decide to adopt about God, or any other matter, although we cannot in consistency say certain things and remain within it. We are free to commit ourselves to what we like, and in the end the decision whether to join, remain within or leave the Christian community is a matter for the individual. Whether the decision is a right one or not can only depend on whether Christianity is true. The fact that there is a Christian community with rules for what can and cannot be said within it is totally irrelevant to this basic question. People do make individual commitments, even if the commitments are to 'forms of life' or 'systems', and if the commitments cannot be said to be true or false, an element of arbitrariness must enter in.

5

The rationality of commitments

Commitments and reasons

The view that commitments as such cannot be justified, and that a justification of anything must presuppose a previous commitment, is influential in many areas of philosophy. It results in the dethroning of the notion of a reason, so that it is no longer all-embracing. Instead it becomes relative to a particular commitment. What counts as a good reason within one commitment may be regarded as a bad one in another, and no reason at all in the third. Reasons cannot be neutral between commitments, since it is a commitment itself which gives them life as reasons. It is a result of this view that it becomes impossible to understand, let alone discuss, the basic questions of a religion before one has committed oneself to that religion. If I do not have a religious faith, I will not appreciate the reasons which believers have for their faith. What counts as a reason within their commitment will not within mine.

This view is not the same as the undoubted (and uninteresting) truth that if two rational people disagree about something, they will each have different reasons for their opinions. The view which we are considering would go much further. Not only, it would claim, do people differ in the reasons they have for their beliefs and actions, but they can differ in what they are willing to *count as* a reason. R. M. Hare maintains a similar position in his well-known article about what he calls 'bliks'. These are beliefs or attitudes which are compatible with any state of affairs. Hare gives as an example the belief that everything which happened, happened by pure chance. As he points out, this belief would make an enormous difference to the lives of those who held it, even though they could not be *asserting* anything different from those who did not share their belief. Both would agree about what actually happened. One group would plan for the future, the other would not. He says: 'This is the sort of difference that there is between those who really believe in God, and those who really disbelieve in Him.'[1] For our present purposes, however, the significant passage is where Hare says, 'It is by our "bliks" that we decide what is and what is not explanation.'[2] In other words, our adoption of a 'blik' (like that of a 'decision of principle' in Hare's system of moral philosophy) takes place within a vacuum. Nothing can count for or against it. It is only when we have a 'blik' that we can see certain things as explanations and reasons. To adopt a 'blik' is to enter a fundamental commitment which is the source of all such notions. This view about the role of reason has analogies with views put forward by Wittgenstein about conceptual systems. For Hare the individual's attitude decides what will count as a reason. For Wittgenstein the conceptual system determines it. Neither allow that reasons could have general validity and that an individual or a system could be wrong about what a good reason for belief was. Wittgenstein is particularly concerned with this kind of issue in the notes which he wrote at the very end of his life on the problems of knowledge and certainty. He says:

All testing, all confirmation and disconfirmation of a hypothesis takes place already within a system. And this system is not a more or less arbitrary and doubtful point of departure for all our arguments: no it belongs to the essence of what we call an argument. The system is not so much the point of departure, as the element in which arguments have their life.[3]

[1] R. M. Hare, 'Theology and Falsification', in *New Essays in Philosophical Theology*, ed. A. N. Flew and A. Macintyre.
[2] *Ibid.* p. 101.
[3] Wittgenstein, *On Certainty*, § 105.

The system is, in fact, the way we think, and Wittgenstein is particularly concerned as to what can be said when two different systems clash. Can we say that one is wrong? Is there any objective truth against which a system can be measured? He asks, for example (writing nearly twenty years before the first men set foot on the moon), what reply could be made to a tribe who believed that people sometimes go to the moon, and yet agreed that there were no ordinary means of getting there. Perhaps, Wittgenstein suggests, that might be how they interpret their dreams. They have a different way of thinking, and all Wittgenstein can conclude is that we would feel 'intellectually very distant' from such people. His point is that it will be impossible to appeal to any neutral standard which will enable us to prove to them that their system is mistaken. It is not enough for us to appeal to empirical evidence because in their system of thought such evidence is not important. We would therefore be begging the question if we quoted such evidence to show them their error. What is at issue is precisely the question whether what *we* count as good evidence is relevant. As Wittgenstein says: 'To say: in the end we can only adduce such grounds as *we* hold to be grounds is to say nothing at all.'[1] In the same way Wittgenstein is very suspicious of the expression 'true or false'.[2] He considers that it is like saying 'it tallies with the facts or it doesn't', and he maintains 'the very thing that is in question is what "tallying" is here'. Indeed, we might add, it could well be that what is a fact is in question as well.

The trouble is that we can only argue from the standpoint of our own assumptions about the world, and these may be disputed by the person we are arguing with. If, for example, we are arguing with the tribe which believes that people go to the moon in their dreams, we may feel inclined to say that it must be possible to prove them right or wrong by some

[1] *Ibid.* § 599.
[2] *Ibid.* § 199.

kind of experiment. We could be relying on our belief that an empirical proposition can be tested.[1] This in itself is an assumption and even if the members of the tribe accepted it, there is still the question 'What *counts* as its test?'.[2] What a contemporary scientist would call an acceptable test may be very different from what tribesmen who thought in a totally alien way would allow. To say to them that we have checked their assertions scientifically and found them false would be merely to re-affirm our faith in scientific method. The snag is of course that there is nothing else we can do to convince them, or so Wittgenstein believes. He considers what would happen if we met people who consulted an oracle instead of a physicist. He wonders if it is possible to regard it as wrong for them to consult an oracle and says: 'If we call this "wrong" aren't we using our language-game as a base from which to *combat* theirs?'[3] In fact, he thinks that we can only shout slogans at each other. There is no neutral, mutually acceptable ground where the contest can take place. Everything we say to them must, in the last resort, presuppose our way of looking at things. If people with commitments which are fundamentally opposed meet each other, argument is fruitless. Argument can only take on life *within* a commitment. Between commitments, it can only be employed by relying on the very assumptions which are in question. Wittgenstein says:

Where two principles really do meet which cannot be reconciled with one another, then each man declares the other a fool and a heretic. I said 'combat' the other man – but wouldn't I give him *reasons*? Certainly: but how far do they go? At the end of reasons comes *persuasion* (Think what happens when missionaries convert natives).[4]

Reasons may be totally ineffective. What I count as a

[1] Wittgenstein, *On Certainty*, § 109.
[2] *Ibid.* § 110.
[3] *Ibid.* § 609.
[4] *Ibid.* §§ 611–12.

reason may not appear to be any reason at all to my opponent. Wittgenstein's reference to missionaries shows that he does have religious commitment in mind. He is saying that it is impossible to give any grounds for religious belief which can lay claim to objectivity, since objectivity is in principle impossible. It is necessary to rely on other methods for conversion. I suggested earlier that Wittgenstein ignored the propositional element in religious commitment. It can now be seen that he is not singling out religion for this treatment. He is treating branches of science in the same way. If he says that religious belief is not the kind of thing which can be true or false, he also says the same thing of the beliefs of physicists. We can talk of something being true or false within the system of physics. This provides the context in which our experiments can take place. Physics itself, however, cannot be said to be justified or unjustified, and those who adhere to a different system cannot simply be said to be wrong. We have no grounds for saying so, which do not derive from our own system. The propositions of physics cannot be called 'true' if this implies that they have a validity which extends beyond our system of physics. For us to insist that they are valid even for those who reject them is merely to reaffirm *our* commitment to them. In the same way, Wittgenstein's refusal to accept a propositional element in religious commitment stemmed from his denial that there is any content in the claim that the pictures entertained by religious believers are valid for those in a non-religious 'form of life'. The claim would not affect the latter in any way. Their lives would remain unchanged.

As a result, Wittgenstein can compare the situation where a child is told by an adult (in 1950) that he had been on the moon, and the one where a child is being taught about God. He faces the probability that a child will not accept our word that the men had not been on the moon, and that 'no-one has ever been on the moon: the moon is a long way off, and it is impossible to climb up there or fly there'.[1] Wittgenstein asks what reply we could make to the child if he insists that we may be wrong, and that perhaps there is a way of getting there which we do not know. Clearly Wittgenstein thinks that there is nothing more we can say. Such a child is in fact challenging our whole system of thought. Wittgenstein points out that a child does not ordinarily stick to such a position and is soon convinced 'by what we tell him seriously'. The child accepts our way of thinking. Wittgenstein then asks: 'Isn't this altogether like the way one can instruct a child to believe in God, or that none exists, and it will accordingly be able to produce apparently telling grounds for the one or the other?'[2]

A child can be instructed in a theistic or an atheistic system of thought, just as he can be taught modern science or be brought up to believe in oracles. One can teach a system, but it seems that one cannot justify it to someone who challenges it. Wittgenstein realises[3] that this seems to suggest that there is no objective truth, and he faces the objection that it is surely true or false that someone has been on the moon. He stresses, however, that we can only answer this from the point of view of *our* system. We can only decide whether there is evidence for or against someone's having been on the moon by using our notion of what counts as evidence. Since another system may not accept our 'evidence', what we say cannot necessarily be considered to have any application outside our system of thought. Wittgenstein then answers the original question about men on the moon. He says in a passage which reads rather strangely now:

If we are thinking within our system, then it is certain that no-one has ever been on the moon. Not merely is nothing of the sort ever seriously

[1] Wittgenstein, *On Certainty*, § 106.
[2] *Ibid.* § 107.
[3] *Ibid.* § 108.

reported to us by reasonable people, but our whole system of physics forbids us to believe it. For this demands answers to the questions 'How did he overcome the force of gravity?', 'How could he live without an atmosphere?' and a thousand others which could not be answered.

This passage is worth consideration, because it prompts the question what, if anything, has happened to our system of physics now that man has been shown to be capable of reaching the moon. A lot depends on the precise force of 'could not' when Wittgenstein specifies questions which, given our system of physics, he thinks *could not* be answered. It looks as if he is saying that it is a logical truth that our system could not answer these questions, and that if we did answer them, our whole way of thinking would be altered. We would be adopting a different system. The questions he gives as examples, however, look like empirical difficulties which could be (as they were) met by an advance in technology. Even when Wittgenstein wrote this passage some scientists were well on the way to a solution of the problems involved. Whether the questions posed by Wittgenstein could be answered within the existing system of physics or not, crucial questions are raised about the role of new discoveries to existing systems of thought. Is it possible for such systems to be proved *wrong*? If our whole system of physics still forbade us to believe that anyone had ever been on the moon, would we not now have to reject it? The trouble is that we may very well refuse to accept that someone had been on the moon, if to admit it meant rejecting our whole system of physics. We might continue to maintain that such a thing was impossible.

The views of T. S. Kuhn

The views of T. S. Kuhn[1] on the status of scientific theories have recently been very influential. They run parallel to

[1] Kuhn, *The Structure of Scientific Revolutions.*

Wittgenstein's at many points, and challenge the notion that scientific theories can aspire to any objectivity. Kuhn suggests that there is no such thing in the field of science. The practice of 'normal' science depends on commitment to what he vaguely terms 'paradigms' which provide scientists with the conceptual equipment by means of which they view the world. Without a paradigm, Kuhn claims, a scientist cannot distinguish the relevant and the significant from the irrelevant and the insignificant. Without some sort of theory he cannot even conduct experiments. Indeed, what is a fact for one paradigm may not exist at all for another. Kuhn says: 'Successive paradigms tell us different things about the population of the universe and about that population's behaviour. They differ, that is, about such questions as the existence of subatomic particles, the materiality of light and the conservation of heat or of energy.'[1]

When a scientist transfers his allegiance from one paradigm to another, Kuhn maintains that his whole way of looking at the world is altered, and, in a sense, the world is different for him. Kuhn gives as an example the transition from Newtonian to Einsteinian mechanics as illustrating 'the scientific revolution as a displacement of the conceptual network, through which scientists view the world'.

Because of this shift of vision different theories are said by Kuhn to be 'incommensurable'. Their content cannot be compared. What plays an important role in one theory may not even exist according to another. It follows that there can be no question of translating the claims of one theory into the language of another. They will to a greater or lesser extent fail to correspond with each other. It is not possible, either, to judge each by means of a neutral language. Kuhn denies the very possibility of comparing theories by means of a basic vocabulary 'consisting', as he puts it, 'entirely of words which are attached to nature in ways that are un-

[1] *Ibid.* p. 102.

problematic, and, to the extent necessary, independent of theory'. He explains as follows:

In the transition from one theory to the next words change their meanings or conditions of applicability in subtle ways. Though most of the same signs are used before and after a revolution – e.g. force, mass, element, compound, cell – the ways in which some of them attach to nature has somehow changed. Successive theories are thus, we say, incommensurable.[1]

Immediately the question how adherents of one theory can ever understand a different one raises itself. Will they not, as a matter of logic, be trapped in their way of looking at the world, so that while their own theory is invulnerable to criticism, they cannot even understand what the proponents of other theories are saying? In views such as that of Kuhn's it is often not entirely clear whether it is just very difficult for different groups to understand each other's language or whether it is actually logically impossible. Current jargon about 'communication breakdown' (and Kuhn himself uses this term)[2] often obscures this important distinction. It is never suggested that it is logically impossible to learn the language of a particular theory or way of looking at the world. That would be obvious nonsense. What is sometimes thought logically impossible is to learn the language of a new theory, while remaining loyal to one's own. There is an obvious parallel here with D. Z. Phillips' view that loss of Christian belief implies finding the whole Christian form of life meaningless, and indeed with the whole Wittgensteinian notion that understanding a way of life cannot be separated from adopting it. In the same way Kuhn tends to the view that it is impossible to understand a theory completely without actually subscribing to it. It thus seems to become impossible to understand two conflicting theories

[1] Kuhn, 'Reflections on my Critics', in *Criticism and the Growth of Knowledge* (ed. I. Lakatos and A. Musgrave), p. 266.
[2] *Ibid.* p. 277.

simultaneously, although if different theories are totally in-commensurable it becomes wholly mysterious how one could ever tell whether two theories were in competition or not. Kuhn asserts that scientists holding different theories 'see different things and see them in different relations one to the other'.[1] He continues:

That is why a law that cannot even be demonstrated to one group of scientists may occasionally seem intuitively obvious to another. Equally, it is why, before they can hope to communicate fully, one group or the other must experience the conversion that we have been calling a paradigm shift.

Kuhn compares such a shift to the switch we make when we see the duck-rabbit drawing first as a duck and then as a rabbit. We cannot see it both as the duck and as the rabbit simultaneously. This all makes it look as if he is making our inability to understand theories we do not hold a matter of logical impossibility. In a later article[2] it is clear that he is reluctant to go this far, and he considers how one scientist who uses terms like 'element' and 'compound' in one way might set about grasping another's use. 'Each,' Kuhn says, 'may try to discover what the other would see and say when presented with a stimulus to which his visual and verbal response would be different.' It is clear that Kuhn is merely emphasising the empirical difficulty of seeing the world as another scientist sees it. However, even here, there is still more than a whiff of the logical thesis. Kuhn still hankers after the view that to understand a theory fully must be to subscribe to it. He says:

Exploring an alternative theory by techniques like those outlined above, one is likely to find that one is already using it (as one suddenly notes that one is thinking in, not translating out of, a foreign language). At no point was one aware of having reached a decision, made a choice. That sort of change is, however, conversion . . .

[1] Kuhn, *The Structure of Scientific Revolutions*, p. 149.
[2] Kuhn, 'Reflections on my Critics', p. 277.

To understand, one does not have to be converted, but the two are clearly still closely linked in Kuhn's mind. They are no longer identified, as he has become aware that this must involve him in saying that becoming committed to a theory is a blind and therefore arbitrary process. There must, he thinks, be a possibility of real choice between theories. How this is to be made is another matter.

Like Wittgenstein, Kuhn emphasises that the basic commitment is outside the realm of reason. Just because paradigms set the standards, there is nothing in science to which an appeal can be made if a choice between paradigms becomes necessary. Kuhn says:

To the extent ... that two scientific schools disagree about what is a problem and what a solution, they will inevitably talk through each other when debating the relative merits of their respective paradigms. In the partially circular arguments that regularly result, each paradigm will be shown to satisfy more or less the criteria it dictates for itself and to fall short of a few of those dictated by its opponent.[1]

Even in science, it seems, there can be no room for any sort of rational detachment. Indeed, Kuhn's position is that such an outlook is impossible in principle. Reason follows in the train of commitment, it cannot judge it. It follows that a scientist can only change from allegiance to one paradigm to allegiance to another as a result of non-scientific considerations. Kuhn observes: 'Something must make at least a few scientists feel that the new proposal is on the right track, and sometimes it is only personal and inarticulate considerations that can do that.'[2]

Like all relativists and subjectivists in every field, Kuhn finds it difficult to be consistent in his resistance to objectivity. His reference to the proposal being 'on the right track' indicates that he cannot shake himself entirely free of notions concerning external standards of right and wrong. Indeed,

[1] Kuhn, *The Structure of Scientific Revolutions*, p. 108.
[2] *Ibid*, p. 157.

it is difficult to see how a scientist could work unless he thought he was measuring his findings against independent standards. The tenor of Kuhn's thesis is strongly against such a view. He explicitly refers to the scientist's transfer of allegiance from paradigm to paradigm, as a 'conversion experience', and considers that such a decision can only be made 'on faith'.[1] He is in fact comparing the adoption of a paradigm with conversion to a religion, and clearly assumes that reason can even in principle play no part in the latter. As a result, it is impossible, according to Kuhn, to call any scientific theory 'wrong'. There is no neutral consideration to which we could appeal. Indeed, since the concepts adopted as a result of commitment to different paradigms themselves differ, we would be in the Wittgensteinian position of not being able to understand fully (if at all) those who disagree with us. It would, on Kuhn's view, be almost impossible to formulate the disagreement. He considers what happens when a new view gains currency, while an old view is still adhered to by some. The situation is not unlike the confrontation imagined by Wittgenstein between those who put their trust in physics, and those who believe in oracles. The difference is that Kuhn is envisaging a controversy between two groups of sophisticated scientists, one of which insists on clinging to the old-fashioned view. Kuhn says of the latter:

Even they, we cannot say, are wrong. Though the historian can always find men who were unreasonable to resist for as long as they did, he will not find a point at which resistance becomes illogical or unscientific. At most he may wish to say that the man who continues to resist after his whole profession has been converted has *ipso facto* ceased to be a scientist.[2]

We might wonder in what sense they could be thought *unreasonable* to hold out, as the question whether to adopt the new paradigm is not one which, according to Kuhn, could be settled by rational considerations. It looks as if

[1] *Idem.*
[2] *Ibid.* p. 118.

Kuhn is still smuggling in notions that should be alien to his relativist approach. He says: 'Because scientists are reasonable men, one or another argument will ultimately persuade many of them. But there is no single argument that can or should persuade them.'[1] Kuhn should make up his mind. Either a change of paradigm is subject to reason or it is not. If it is, then it is possible to talk in terms of 'arguments', and of scientists being 'reasonable'. In that case, however, some arguments will be better than others, and it will be possible to think of one view being more correct – or more nearly right – than the other. If Kuhn does not wish to admit this much, he must completely rule out talk of reasonableness and of arguments. If reason is to have no place, then anything could count as an argument. That, however, is to say that the very notion of an argument in this context must be a meaningless one. As a result, no factor which is seen to make for paradigm change should be thought preferable to any other. Kuhn himself mentions several such factors.[2] Among them are 'idiosyncrasies of autobiography and personality', and Kuhn remarks that even the nationality or prior reputation of the innovator and his teachers can be important. If these were the kind of considerations which produced paradigm change, any suggestion that scientists were reasonable men would be ludicrous. Because Kuhn cannot allow that any reasons for the rejection of an old paradigm and the acceptance of a new one might be independent of the two paradigms, he has to deny that a change in commitment to a paradigm can be a rational procedure. Any method of producing a change is as good as any other. Such a view has even more impracticable results when applied to other fields. Kuhn draws an explicit analogy between scientific and political revolutions. He sketches out a revolutionary situation in political terms, where one party is trying to

[1] Kuhn, *The Structure of Scientific Revolutions*, p. 157.
[2] *Ibid.* p. 152.

E

defend the old institutional framework, whereas the revolutionaries are committed to the reconstruction of a society in a new institutional form. Kuhn continues:

Because they differ about the institutional matrix within which political change is to be achieved and evaluated, because they acknowledge no supra-institutional framework for the adjudication of revolutionary difference, the parties to a revolutionary conflict must finally resort to the techniques of mass persuasion, often including force.[1]

One may perhaps wonder why Kuhn did not examine the possibility of producing paradigm change in science by force. It is hard to see what arguments he could produce against such a policy. He has accepted that 'non-scientific' factors will be instrumental in making scientists change their basic commitments to paradigms. It is not clear how he would distinguish between different non-scientific factors and find some more acceptable than others. Either he must agree that there is some standard against which such factors can be judged or he must acknowledge that anything goes. For instance, Lakatos has asserted:

If even in science, there is no other way of judging a theory but by assessing the number, faith, and vocal energy of its supporters, then this must be even more so in the social sciences: truth lies in power. Thus Kuhn's position would indicate, no doubt unintentionally, the basic political credo of contemporary religious maniacs ('student revolutionaries').[2]

Not surprisingly, Kuhn wishes to reject this charge and puts forward a subtle modification of his former views. He does so by insisting that there *are* many good reasons for choosing one theory rather than another, such as the accuracy, scope, simplicity and fruitfulness of the various theories.[3] He says:

[1] *Ibid.* p. 92.
[2] Lakatos and Musgrave (eds.), *Criticism and the Growth of Knowledge*, p. 93.
[3] *Ibid.* p. 261.

What I am denying then is neither the existence of good reasons nor that these reasons are of the sort usually described. I am, however, insisting that such reasons constitute values to be used in making choices rather than rules of choice. Scientists who share them may nevertheless make different choices in the same concrete situation.[1]

Kuhn goes on to point out that different individuals may place different weight on the various values in cases of value-conflict, and that scientists anyway do not all apply them in the same way. It follows that there will be considerable variation in different scientists' judgment. Kuhn insists that the judgment will not be arbitrary, although he does not explain how it can avoid being so. There is no suggestion, though, that the 'good reasons' Kuhn mentions have anything other than a sociological significance. They are the kind of things which scientists happen to think important, although if they did not, science would not cease to exist. As he blandly says, 'if they did not hold values like these, their disciplines would develop very differently'.

These 'good reasons', therefore, will not provide any path to truth. Rejection of them will not involve any mistake or error. It would merely be to step outside the scientific community, as it happens to be at the time. A good reason seems merely to be what the members of the scientific community happen to attach importance to, and there is no restriction on what they can value. He maintains that 'the responsibility for applying shared scientific values must be left to the specialists' group'. He continues: 'If the specialists' group behaves as a mob, renouncing its normal values, then science is already past saving.' Clearly, however, there can be no reason why they should not do just this. Kuhn cannot say they are wrong, because he has left himself with no standards to appeal to beyond those which scientists themselves recognise. If they stop thinking that there are good reasons for choosing one theory rather than another, and start using

[1] *Ibid.* p. 262.

non-rational means of persuasion, all Kuhn can say is that the nature of science has changed. He may in fact be able to say that it has so radically altered that it is no longer 'science', but that would be a purely descriptive point. 'Science' cannot for Kuhn be in any way a normative term, although his remark about science getting past saving suggests he may not have fully accepted this.

Kuhn is evidently unhappy about this interpretation of the consequences of his position:

No part of the argument here or in my book implies that scientists may choose any theory they like so long as they agree in their choice and thereafter enforce it. Most of the puzzles of normal science are directly presented by nature, and all involve nature indirectly. Though different solutions have been received as valid at different times, nature cannot be forced into an arbitrary set of conceptual boxes.[1]

This sounds all well and good, but it hardly accords with Kuhn's belief that there are *no* neutral data waiting for the interpretation of the scientist. He thinks that it is impossible to talk of 'nature' independently of a particular theory, and that one theory will deal with data which are totally different from those of another theory. He insists that after a revolution scientists work in a different world, and this, together with his belief that scientific revolutions can only be explained in causal terms, suggests that any talk of nature influencing theory-choice must be ruled out. There may well be a conception of nature within a particular theory, and as a result problems may be seen as being presented by nature, but this is beside the point. No-one questions that, after commitment to a theory, scientists may act in an apparently rational manner. What is at issue is whether it is possible to talk of scientists making a rational choice between theories. Unless one can conceive of nature independently of any theory and one can see how well or badly a particular theory fits neutral data, such a choice must be logically

[1] Kuhn, 'Reflections on my Critics', p. 263.

impossible. According to Kuhn, 'nature' in one theory will be totally different from 'nature' in another. To suggest, as he does in the passage we are considering, that scientists have at different times been attempting to explain precisely the same thing ('nature') is to go dead against this view, since it must involve him in characterising nature in a way not dependent on any theory.

Whatever hesitations Kuhn may have when he faces the consequences of his views, Feyerabend has none. He is quite prepared to admit the 'irrationality' of science. He should perhaps rather be saying that science is not the kind of thing which can be rational or irrational, reasonable or unreasonable, since to talk of irrationality in a certain area is to presuppose that there are standards of rationality which can be applied to it, and this is precisely what Feyerabend wishes to deny. He is in complete agreement with the need for Kuhn's concept of the 'incommensurability' of theories. He agrees that 'succeeding paradigms can be evaluated only with difficulty and that they may be altogether incomparable'.[1] We may note here the familiar ambivalence between what is empirically difficult and what is logically impossible. In fact, later on Feyerabend says quite firmly of incommensurable theories that 'their content cannot be compared'.[2] He stresses that there is no possibility of making any judgment of verisimilitude, except within a theory. He boldly asserts: 'What remains are aesthetic judgments, judgments of taste, and our own subjective wishes.'[3] Feyerabend is firmly grasping the nettle. If scientific theories cannot be true or false, an obvious 'explanation' why we choose one rather than another might be that we just feel like doing so. A scientist's attachment to a particular theory would then be as

[1] Feyerabend, 'Consolation for the Specialist', in *Criticism and the Growth of Knowledge* (ed. I. Lakatos and A. Musgrave), p. 219.
[2] *Ibid.* p. 227.
[3] *Ibid.* p. 228.

unremarkable as his taste for toffee. Just as he need not produce reasons for the latter (a taste for toffee cannot be criticised for being irrational), he need not justify his commitment to the theory. The preferences of scientists for one theory rather than another will tell us nothing about them, and nothing about the world, as all pretence that scientific theories describe and explain nature has been abandoned. Feyerabend emphasises that the sciences are our own creation. He continues:

It is good to be constantly reminded of the fact that science as we know it today is not inescapable and that we may construct a world in which it plays no role whatever ... What better reminder is there than the realization that the choice between theories which are sufficiently general to provide us with a comprehensive world view and which are empirically disconnected may become a matter of taste? That the choice of our basic cosmology may become a matter of taste?[1]

Feyerabend goes on to indicate how such things as poems which are not the kind of thing which can be true or false can nevertheless be critically scrutinised. They can, he says, 'be compared in grammar, sound, structure, imagery, and can be evaluated on such a basis'. He continues: 'Every poet who is not completely irrational composes, improves, argues until he finds the correct formulation of what he wants to say. Would it not be marvellous if this process played a role in the sciences also?'

Presumably Feyerabend thinks that a scientist should in a similar way try to find the '"correct" formulation of what he wants to say'. This, however, begs a great many questions about what a correct formulation would be. Since scientists usually think they are talking about the world and not themselves, the most natural interpretation of 'correctness' in this context would have to rely on some external notion of truth. For Feyerabend, however, the test of correctness is independent of the relation of the theory

[1] *Idem.*

to the world; the test is whether the theory adequately reflects a particular scientist's wishes or not. Does Feyerabend then think there is any limitation on what a scientist might want to say, if he can no longer be considered to be aiming at truth? His reference to possible irrationality in a poet suggests that he thinks that there are certain standards to which a poet, and anyone else in the arts, should conform. He thinks that the situation in science is similar. If there are standards (of the kind which Feyerabend mentions in connection with poetry), it follows that it is true that there are. The idea of extra-theoretical truth is appearing again. There are external criteria which can be used to judge artistic productions and scientific theories, and they exist independently of people's recognition of them. If, however, Feyerabend wishes to make such standards as subjective as tastes, something is a standard for someone only if he thinks it is. My standards may not be your standards. Clearly anything could then be thought to be a standard, and the result would be anarchy in both the arts and the sciences. Certainly the notion of irrationality would be ruled out, as we could have no idea of what it would be to be rational.

It looks, therefore, as if Feyerabend has a choice between the total anarchy of subjectivism or an appeal to objective standards, which raises again the very notion of truth which he is trying to attack. Even though he may have been relying implicitly on the idea of fixed aesthetic standards, his denial of the possibility of making judgments of verisimilitude in science still represents a significant attack on generally accepted views about the status of science. Mere demonstration of the necessity of some settled criteria for the construction of theories may still quite easily allow for the impossibility of comparing the content of succeeding theories and therefore the impossibility of talking of truth, at least in the sense of any kind of correspondence with reality.

An examination of the general context of Feyerabend's remarks makes it clear that he does not regard aesthetic standards as providing much of an obstacle to our own subjective wishes. He may have felt the need to soften the impact of the 'epistemological anarchism' which he has explicitly embraced, but it is clear that in the end he thinks a scientific theory can be whatever scientists want it to be. His general attitude is made quite clear when he remarks that the attempt to judge cosmologies by their content may have to be given up. He continued: 'Such a development, far from being undesirable, changes science from a stern and demanding mistress into an attractive and yielding courtesan who tries to anticipate every wish of her lover.'[1] Even allowing for the flippancy of this remark, the inherent subjectivism is obvious. Scientists, according to Feyerabend, can quite literally believe and say what they like. The concepts of truth and of reason in science have been sacrificed at a great cost. The alternative must, at least as Feyerabend presents it, be one where arbitrary tests and preferences determine not only what is said but what can in principle be said.

In another article, Feyerabend denies that there can be universal standards of truth and rationality, and hence that there can be any general standard for what should count as error. He continues:

We can only speak of what does, or does not, seem appropriate when viewed from a particular and restricted point of view, different views, temperaments, attitudes giving rise to different judgements and different methods of approach. Such an *anarchistic epistemology* ... is not only a better means for improving knowledge or of understanding history. It is also more appropriate for a free man to use than are its rigorous and 'scientific' alternatives.[2]

This clarion call to freedom may appear stirring, but it is

[1] Feyerabend, 'Consolation for the Specialist', p. 229.
[2] Feyerabend, 'Against Method: Outline of an Anarchistic Theory of Knowledge', *Minnesota Studies in the Philosophy of Science* (1970), IV, 21.

ironic that Feyerabend himself shows that he cannot embrace the full consequences of his position. He wishes to retain the concept of knowledge and the notion of *improving* our knowledge. But if nothing is true, there is nothing to know, and certainly nothing further to find out.

Kuhn's references to 'conversion' and 'faith' in a scientific context indicate that he would apply his analysis to religion as well as to science. He obviously assumes that in denying any place for reason in the making of a fundamental commitment he is bringing science into line with religion. His approach, like that of Wittgenstein and Feyerabend, must ultimately involve an attack on the very possibility of rationality. Even to suggest this as a criticism is to invite the accusation that the whole question is being begged. It is because neither Wittgenstein nor Kuhn can accept the idea of an all-embracing rationality, which can adjudicate between ultimate commitments, that they adopt the position they do. We cannot therefore use as an argument against them the fact that their views have unfortunate consequences for the notion of rationality.

Indeed Kuhn, while making it clear that he agrees with much Feyerabend says, criticises him for describing his argument as a defence of irrationality in science. Instead, he says, 'I would describe it, together with my own, as an attempt to show that existing theories of rationality are not quite right and that we must readjust or change them to explain why science works as it does.' Kuhn is thus trying to elucidate what we mean by rationality rather than to argue that there is no such thing or to defend irrationality (indeed to provoke arguments in favour of irrationality seems a somewhat self-contradictory exercise). Nevertheless it is important to stress just how fundamental an attack is being made on the assumptions with which we normally operate. It is being claimed that all the most important decisions we make in life – whether in the spheres of religion, of ethics, of science, or of politics – must in the last resort be regarded as arbitrary. Alternatively they must be regarded as subject to causal factors of which we may very well be unaware, or which, even if we are aware of them, we will be unable to control. If it were possible to control them, we would immediately have to decide whether we should do so. The question whether there were reasons for our choice would then once more arise.

Kuhn and truth

In the field of science, Kuhn suggests: 'Truth may, like "proof", be a term with only intra-theoretic applications.' He contrasts his position with that of many philosophers of science:

They wish to compare theories as representations of nature, as statements about 'what is really out there'. Granting that neither theory of a historical pair is true, they nonetheless seek a sense in which the later is a better approximation to the truth. I believe nothing of that sort can be found.[1]

Kuhn recognises that this position lays him open to a charge of relativism, and admits that in one sense of the term he may be a relativist. He nevertheless claims that in another sense he is not one, since he believes that scientific development is evolutionary. 'For me,' he says, 'scientific development is, like biological evolution, unidirectional and irreversible. One scientific theory is not as good as another for doing what scientists normally do.' Since Kuhn denies the possibility of any neutral language with which to compare theories, it remains very unclear how, given his assumptions, he or anyone else can tell whether science is evolutionary or not. If to talk of evolution is to suggest that science is continually improving in some way, it must be

[1] Kuhn, 'Reflections on my Critics', p. 226.

possible to compare the theories to see if this is so. Yet this is precisely what, with his emphasis on the 'incommensurability' of theories, he denies is possible. It also suggests that we have some standard (such as truth) with which to decide what counted as an improvement. The alternative is that Kuhn merely supposes evolution in science to be some kind of blind and pointless process, so that if theory X comes after theory Y in the same scientific speciality, it must be thought of as having evolved from it. It is clear that Kuhn has more than this in mind. He believes it to be possible to design a set of criteria to determine which theory was older. The examples which he gives, such as 'maximum accuracy of predictions, degree of specialization' and 'number (but not scope) of concrete problem solutions' all carry with them the flavour of an ever-growing sophistication towards a definite goal. Without the concept of truth it is very difficult to say what the goal could be. Indeed, Kuhn seems to want to say both that science is developing in one direction and that there could not in principle be any direction for science as such to go.

It is not surprising that Kuhn feels that in a sense he is a relativist and in a sense he is not. He wants to retain all the benefits which the concept of truth provides while saying that there is no such thing as truth external to theories. It is not just words such as 'evolution' and 'development' which depend on the existence of standards by which scientific theories can be judged. The very notion of scientific 'progress' would obviously collapse if we had no criteria with which to decide what should count as progress.

Kuhn does not seem to realise this, although he is dimly aware of some of the problems which arise once he cuts out talk of the truth (or approximation to it) of scientific theories. He denies that scientists discover the truth about nature or approach ever closer to the truth. He goes on to say:

Unless, as one of my critics suggests, we simply define the approach to truth as the result of what scientists do, we cannot recognise progress towards that goal. Rather we must explain why science – our surest example of sound knowledge – progresses as it does, and we must first find out how, in fact, it does progress.[1]

Kuhn's answer to the problem he poses is 'that the explanation must, in the final analysis, be psychological or sociological'.[2] However, a more fundamental question than why science progresses is what possible grounds Kuhn could have for talking about 'progress' once he scraps talk about progress towards the truth. To echo what he himself says, unless we define scientific progress as merely what scientists do, we cannot talk of progress at all. Kuhn seems to think it is possible to have 'progress' even when it is not progress in any direction. This is absurd. Even more curious is his assertion that science is 'our surest example of sound knowledge'. It is a fundamental and very elementary point about the concept of knowledge that we can only know what is true. If I know that it is raining, then it must be raining. It follows that if there is no such thing as truth, there can as a matter of logic be no such thing as knowledge.

At the end of *The Structure of Scientific Revolutions* (p. 170) Kuhn simultaneously denies that there is such a thing as truth and goes on talking in terms of 'knowledge'. He says that there is no need to think of science having a goal and continues:

Can we not account for both science's existence and its success in terms of evolution from the community's state of knowledge at any given time? Does it really help to imagine that there is some one full, objective, true account of nature and that the proper measure of scientific achievement is the extent to which it brings us closer to that ultimate goal? If we can learn to substitute evolution-from-what-we-do-know for evolution-

[1] Kuhn, 'Logic of Discovery or Psychology of Research?' in *Criticism and the Growth of Knowledge* (ed. I. Lakatos and A. Musgrave), p. 20.
[2] *Ibid.* p. 21.

toward-what-we-wish-to-know, a number of vexing problems may vanish in the process.[1]

The basic problem is how it is possible to talk of knowledge at all in connection with science, if Kuhn's account is correct. If a 'true' account of nature is in principle impossible, then knowledge must be unattainable. Once again, Kuhn wants to retain the use of a concept which has the concept of truth at its foundation, while kicking away that foundation.

In another passage,[2] Kuhn displays an equally astonishing ambivalence. He wishes to emphasise that the members of a given scientific group will make different choices when faced with alternative theories. He assumes that they will be committed to considering 'such values as accuracy, simplicity, scope and so on', but stresses that 'individual choice will be a function also of personality, education, and the prior pattern of professional research' and remarks that these variables are the province of individual psychology. Kuhn here wants to put forward a view which is in line with his total rejection of the concept of extra-theoretical truth, so that choice between theories must be a matter of psychology, once one has granted the effects of a shared ideology (itself subject to sociological explanation). His reference to a commitment to consider such a value as accuracy does not of itself involve him in any contradiction, because he would deny that he is setting up accuracy as any kind of objective criterion. He is merely pointing out that as a matter of empirical fact, scientists tend to be committed to valuing such things, even though their commitment is not the kind of thing which could itself be rationally justified. So far Kuhn is maintaining a consistent, although controversial, position, but he goes on to say: 'If a decision must be made under circumstances in which even the most deliberate and considered judgment may be wrong, it may be vitally

[1] Kuhn, *The Structure of Scientific Revolutions*, p. 170.
[2] Kuhn, 'Reflections on my Critics', p. 241.

important that different individuals decide in different ways. How else could the group as a whole hedge its bets?'

Kuhn here seems to imply that scientific theories can be true or false. It is impossible to conceive of a theory being wrong or mistaken if there can be no conception of what it would be for it to be correct, or true. It follows that without the concept of truth Kuhn cannot consistently say that any judgment about a scientific theory could be wrong. Any theory must otherwise be on equal terms with any other, and there is no possibility of being mistaken if one plumps for one rather than another. One cannot be wrong, because in this context it is impossible to say what 'being wrong' amounts to. Yet Kuhn seems to think that the absence of external standards for theory choice does not rule out 'wrong' as an inappropriate word but rather makes it all the more likely one will go wrong. In other words, it merely adds to the difficulty a scientist faces. In fact, of course, it transforms the logic of the situation, and makes it impossible to say things which even Kuhn clearly wants (and is forced) to go on saying. His reference to the scientific community 'hedging its bets' powerfully suggests that scientists have an underlying purpose. This could only be the pursuit of truth, which has already been denied them by Kuhn. He has left them nothing to bet on.

6

Relativism and disagreement

The consequences of conceptual relativism

It is intriguing to see how far the views of Kuhn and Feyerabend are from those of the verificationists, who used the
standards of contemporary science to show that religious
utterances were not factually significant. The only truths
were those which could be 'incorporated in the system of
empirical propositions which constitutes science'.[1] Now it
appears that, if Wittgenstein and Kuhn are right, scientific
utterances are in no better state than those of religion.
Indeed it seems as if we have 'progressed' from saying that
only scientific statements can be true to saying that there is
no such thing as truth. If truth and reasoning are made
relative to systems so that what is right in one system can be
wrong in another, and each system has its own set of concepts, we are faced with what can only be termed anarchy.
We have already seen some of the consequences of this kind
of view when examining Wittgenstein's remarks about
religion. There can be no understanding of one system by
those committed to another. As a result, it is not only
impossible in principle to resolve fundamental disagreement,
it is impossible even to formulate it. Kuhn's notion of the
'incommensurability' of different scientific systems has this
result, and we have already seen how on Wittgenstein's
view it becomes impossible for an atheist to disagree with a
Christian. Indeed the very concept of an atheist becomes
puzzling. How can he be denying that God exists, if he
cannot even have the concept of a God? We have already
seen, too, that not only can commitments not be justified,

[1] Ayer, *Language, Truth and Logic* (2nd ed.), p. 120.

but a person logically cannot know to what he is committing himself until he has done so. Emphasis on the relativity of rationality must make any basic commitment totally blind and haphazard.

One can under these circumstances only disagree with those one basically agrees with. Fundamental disagreement must now be seen as mutual incomprehension. Argument with those who do not share our presuppositions becomes logically impossible. We can carry this further. If the concepts of, say, physics are different from those of religion (and this is true by definition if it is accepted that these are two different systems), it is clear that a non-religious physicist and a religious non-physicist would not get very far in a discussion. What, though, would be the position of a religious physicist? It seems as if he could never compare his religion and his physics to see if the one impinged on the other. As a physicist he could not understand his religion, and as a man of religion he could not understand his physics. He would not even be in a position to say that they had nothing to do with each other. How could he know? The result is a totally crazy compartmentalisation of understanding. We are reaching the same type of absurdity as we encountered when trying to find criteria for 'forms of life'. Indeed Wittgenstein's later notion of a system plays a similar role to that of a form of life.

Although we are deriving some peculiar consequences from the attack on the possibility of rationality and objective truth which is implicit in Wittgenstein and Kuhn, it is worth noting that one consequence at least has some currency in popular thinking. This is the view that science and religion involve different ways of thought, dealing with different subjects, and that neither can criticise the other. In particular, religion is invulnerable from attack by scientists. This is doubtless comforting to those who might fear that one day a scientific discovery could show religious beliefs to be false, and it is obviously true that the concerns of science and religion are for the most part different. To assert *a priori*, however, that they can never conflict seems a very large claim to make. Indeed if both are concerned with truth, it is hard to see why they may not find themselves disagreeing about what is true. If, for example, science were ever to prove that determinism was true (and many philosophers would say that this was an empirical matter), it is hard to see how the Christian could continue to preach a doctrine of free-will. Similarly, the Christian view of creation might be thought to fit in more easily with 'big bang' theories of the origin of the universe than theories which suggest that the universe had no beginning. Whether these examples do provide examples of actual areas of conflict is not important. The point is that we can produce cases where it is intelligible that science and religion may each have reasons for saying opposite things. To rule this out by definition could well be merely a subordination of logic to the demands of wishful thinking.

If the possibility of an all-embracing rationality is denied and it is suggested that there are no such things as reasons for commitment, it must follow that it does not matter what we commit ourselves to. Not only will it be impossible (as Hare finds)[1] to produce reasons why a fanatical Nazi is wrong, but we must be forced to admit that it does not matter what he believes. To suggest that it does matter would be to imply that there are reasons for believing one thing rather than another. Even the view that it is important to be committed to *something*, no matter what, is difficult to explain if rationality is relative to systems. What neutral grounds could be produced to show that commitment to *some* system was vital? *Ex hypothesi*, there could be none. If rational grounds could be produced for such a view, there could be no argument to show why grounds could

[1] See Hare, *Freedom and Reason*, p. 184.

not be produced in favour of one commitment and against another.

Why should we be concerned (as we undoubtedly are in everyday life) that people have very different views from our own? It seems that it would not be rational (or irrational) to take any notice of their views. It would presumably be impossible for us even to find them fully intelligible. This cannot be stressed too much, because the point about being unable to say that a Nazi's views are wrong gains much of its force from the fact that we think we know something of what a Nazi's views are. If we cannot find Nazi views comprehensible without being Nazis, we cannot claim they are repugnant. It appears that any argument against the relativity of rationality which assumes that we can find other commitments intelligible could be accused of begging the question.

The absurdities which result from the relativistic views we have been considering clearly indicate that the views must be mistaken. Where have they gone wrong? Why does it seem so attractive to some philosophers to deny that any resolution of basic conflicts is even in principle possible? Clearly they start by observing that in fact it is very difficult to gain any wide agreement in matters of fundamental importance. Ethics and religion provide examples of this. It is a fact of life that there are competing moral systems and competing religions, each making claims to truth. The members of one seem unable to convince the members of another. It is natural, therefore, to conclude that there is no such thing as objective truth. To assert that there is would not be to change anything. Men would still disagree.

Wittgenstein notes that what men consider reasonable and unreasonable varies. He sees that this might indicate there is no 'objective character' here and comments: '*Very* intelligent and well-educated people believe in the story of creation in the Bible, while others hold it as proven false, and the grounds of the latter are well known to the former.'[1] The fact that the same grounds convince some and fail to convince others suggests that it is impossible to lay down standards for what is to be considered reasonable.

In other words the main impetus to relativistic theories comes from the fact of human disagreement. Even basic changes of view are then explained as being the product of causal factors. All this, however, is to concentrate too much on the psychology of individual men. What they do in fact accept or reject ought to be a different question from what is worthy of acceptance or rejection. Why men first became committed to some system may be totally irrelevant to the question of the validity of the system as such. The way someone happens to arrive at a particular view may not be the way the view might be justified. What might make a scientist suddenly relate experimental findings which he had not previously related may have nothing to do with the validity or otherwise of his insight. What makes someone suddenly become converted to a particular religion could be totally irrelevant to general questions about the truth of that religion. The fact, for instance, that a choir sang in an inspiring way at a critical moment could easily be a major cause of a conversion. But one would not suppose that this could justify the new commitment.

Without these basic distinctions, the inevitable result is an obsession with what men do in fact accept and reject. Unless some common denominator is discovered in their beliefs, it will be concluded that the same standards cannot be expected to apply to everyone. If I do not apply the normal standards of rationality to my own thinking, then they cannot be understood to apply to me. The temptation might then well be to say that I am a member of a different 'system' of thought, or 'form of life'. The truth might be that I am obstinate, stupid, or irrational, but on the view under

[1] Wittgenstein, *On Certainty*, § 336.

consideration, such concepts could have no application. If there are no standards other than those I accept, then clearly there is no legitimate way in which any adverse judgment could be passed on me.

Important consequences follow from the distinction between an individual's psychology and the justification for his beliefs. Reference to one must be seen as irrelevant to the other. MacIntyre refers to the fact of Wordsworth being driven into the Church of England by his brother's death, and quite rightly points out that any experience can provide an occasion for conversion. He maintains: 'Only those over-impressed by metaphysics would want to suggest that any logical process is involved.'[1] Clearly that may be true enough of conversion experiences. It is quite questionable how far 'logical processes' are typical of actual thinking. The way a mathematician might see the truth of a theorem might be very different from the way he sets it out to demonstrate it to others. In the same way the absence of any logical process of thought in conversion says nothing as to whether a justification for the newly acquired belief might be forth-coming. MacIntyre says: 'Religious belief is a matter not of argument but of conversion ... There are no reasons to which one can appeal to evade the burden of decision.'[2] The fact, however, that an argument may not convince someone does not necessarily reflect on its validity. Conversion is a matter of psychology: the question of rational justification has to be dealt with on another plane altogether. Just because men do not always think or behave in a rational way, it does not follow that their thoughts and actions cannot be judged against rational standards. Why someone has come to hold certain religious beliefs must be a totally different issue from the question whether what he believes is true. Similarly, the

---

[1] MacIntyre, 'The Logical Status of Religious Beliefs', *Metaphysical Beliefs*, p. 210.
[2] *Ibid.* p. 209.

fact that a justification can in principle be given for a belief does not in any way force anyone to hold that belief. It does raise questions about the extent and nature of human freedom, which we shall consider in a moment.

Typical of the kind of approach to which we are objecting is MacIntyre's attempt to show that everything of importance to religious faith is outside the reach of historical investigation. He maintains for instance, that in asking whether the Resurrection happened, we are not asking anything which, as he puts it, 'future historical investigation might settle'. He considers what would be the result if any new evidence about the Resurrection were found, and says:

Suppose a document alleging the Resurrection to be genuine, certified by Caiaphas, were discovered, those who at present see the Gospels as fabrication would have the same grounds for seeing in the new discovery yet another piece of Christian propaganda. Suppose conversely that a document alleging the Resurrection not to have occurred, certified by the apostles, were discovered. What more probable, Christian scholars would say, than that this kind of anti-Christian forgery should be found?[1]

The whole emphasis of MacIntyre's argument is deliberately laid on how people would probably react in certain circumstances. He does not pause to question whether the reactions would be justifiable. Yet it is surely a legitimate question to pose. The mere fact that certain scholars insisted on dismissing certain evidence would not necessarily show that there was anything wrong with the evidence. It could just as easily be a reflection on their own deep-seated prejudice. It may be very difficult for anyone to be totally objective, particularly when the beliefs which he holds most precious are put into question, but this of itself does not suggest that objectivity is in principle unattainable. The first reaction of a Christian scholar may well be to doubt the authenticity of any document which purported to prove that

[1] *Ibid.* p. 206.

the Resurrection did not occur. It should however be clear that the personal reaction of the scholar is not itself relevant to the document's authenticity. In so far as he is a scholar he should judge the document on its merits, even if it involves his rejecting his religion. Similar considerations apply to any atheist faced with apparent proof of the historicity of the Resurrection. The fact that he is an atheist may make him unable to approach the evidence in a dispassionate manner, but his own belief should be irrelevant to the assessment of the evidence. There is no reason why either a Christian or an atheist must prejudice every issue in favour of their own beliefs. The fact that they may do so does nothing to show that there is no 'truth' in this area. Christian commitment involves a belief that certain things are *true*, and it is a corollary of this that the Christian is concerned with truth. If it becomes apparent that his religion does not, as he thought, embody truth, he will paradoxically remain faithful to the spirit of the religion by repudiating it.

MacIntyre talks of the possibility of historical investigation *settling* whether the Resurrection happened. Much of the difficulty he gets himself into derives from the ambiguity of this word *settle*. When people say that a dispute has been settled, they may mean either of two completely different things. They could be saying that the parties to the dispute have now come to an agreement. The settling, for example, of an industrial dispute may merely involve a compromise which both sides accept. Alternatively the settling of a dispute might involve the demonstration that one view was right, and the opposing view was wrong. Rock brought back from the moon might show that one group of astronomers was right and another group wrong about the nature of the moon. Unfortunately, however, it by no means follows that both sets of astronomers would then agree. Some of them might continue to cling to the discredited theory, and produce progressively more implausible explanations as to why the rock samples did not provide conclusive evidence that they had been wrong. Even though the dispute had been settled in the sense that the truth of the matter was known, it would not have been settled in another sense because agreement would not have been reached. Clearly the reverse is also plausible. The mere fact agreement has been reached need not suggest that the prevailing view is true or that the matter has been settled once and for all. There is no contradiction in supposing that someone might be persuaded to give up a true belief in favour of a false one.

The inability of scholars to agree cannot therefore determine the question of whether historical investigation might 'settle' the problem about the Resurrection. It is quite clear that the sense of 'settle' required here is the one concerning the establishment of the truth or otherwise of certain views. Whether scholarly argument about the issue is brought to an end is another matter. It may be suggested that questions of truth and falsity cannot be dealt with in isolation from what is accepted as true or false, and that the refusal of scholars in a particular field to accept a view as true must be significant. Such disagreement may indeed be a factor which we take into account in trying to discover the truth of a particular matter. Unanimity amongst the experts would be more persuasive than a babble of conflicting voices. But the difficulty or ease with which we can come to a conclusion does not determine whether truth can be talked of where there is disagreement. If complete agreement about something is a necessary condition of our saying it is true (and clearly it could not be a sufficient condition) human knowledge could only be extended at the pace of the slowest, the most stupid or the plain cranky. As long as there were 'flat-earthers' we could not say that it was true that the earth is round. If it were maintained that what is required is agreement among those who are experts about the point at issue, there would clearly be difficulty in deciding who would count as an expert. There would be a temptation only to count as expert those who had reached the conclusion one favoured, and this would be merely to move the whole problem back a stage. In any case, it must clearly be possible for experts to be wrong, so the acknowledgment of someone as an expert would itself solve nothing. It may be objected that this notion of 'being wrong' depends on objectivist assumptions that there are standards against which our beliefs can, at least in principle, be measured. But the very concept of an expert is one which depends on such assumptions. It would be nonsense for the subjectivist to claim that some people have a better claim to knowledge than others, for he himself emphasises that there can be no such thing as knowledge and that each man's judgment is right for him.

The same problems arise over moral disagreement. We have already seen how fundamental disagreement can occur between scientists. Kuhn's relativism sprang largely from this fact. The perplexing occurrence of widespread moral disagreement does not of itself suggest that morality and science are very different kinds of discipline. In both fields individuals and groups often seem to have irreconcilable differences. It seems impossible to settle a dispute. Once again, however, we must recognise that people can reach agreement without necessarily arriving at the truth. Failure to agree, conversely, does not mean that it is impossible to discover the truth. Questions of truth are distinct from questions of individual and group psychology.

R. W. Beardsmore assumes that because men do disagree on basic moral questions there can be no standards of correctness or truth in ethical matters. He thinks that in cases of disagreement there is no established procedure, acceptable to each side, for resolving disputes. This is of course something of a tautology. It merely says that when people fail to agree about what standards are applicable, there are no standards which are acceptable to both sides. Beardsmore says:

We cannot say of a moral dispute (or a moral problem) that it must be solved. To suppose that we can is to ignore the characteristics of moral arguments which distinguish them from empirical arguments. Nevertheless I have also tried to show that I am not thereby committed to the obviously false assertion that no moral dispute is ever capable of solution. To deny that a solution *must* be found is not to say that it *will not* be found, but only that it need not.[1]

Beardsmore had previously claimed that we can say *a priori* how an empirical dispute will turn out.[2] He instances a disagreement between electricians as to whether a length of wire is live, and says that one of them must be wrong. He says: 'There must be some solution to their disagreement. It is precisely in this respect that empirical disagreement differs from moral disagreement.' He has made it easy for himself by picking a very simple empirical disagreement. A fairer comparison could perhaps be made between basic moral disputes and fundamental clashes between rival scientific theories (for example about the origin of the universe). In such cases there is no simple procedure for resolving the dispute. In both morals and science competing views have their adherents who completely refuse to accept what the others say. There seems to be no more guarantee in science than in morals that one side will persuade the other. This, though, seems to be Beardsmore's idea of what would constitute a solution. If he had been less obsessed with the difficulty in getting the parties to a moral dispute to agree, he might have seen that this is irrelevant to whether the dispute is in principle soluble. He has confused the empirical question as to whether a moral dispute will be resolved with the logical question as to whether it is possible to resolve it. Even if it does not make sense to talk of a moral view being

[1] Beardsmore, *Moral Reasoning*, p. 116.
[2] *Ibid.* p. 110.

'right' or 'wrong', it is clear that people can be brought to share the same view. This is all that Beardsmore means by a solution of the dispute. If, however, some moral views are correct and others incorrect, clearly moral problems may be said to be capable of solution, even if agreement is never reached. Agreement about a moral matter would in that case be irrelevant to the solution of the dispute. It would be neither a necessary nor a sufficient condition for a particular view being correct.

We can see in fact that there is the same kind of ambiguity in 'solution' as there is in 'settle'. In one sense a dispute will be solved if the disputants agree, and clearly that may or may not happen. In the other sense, it is a matter of logic whether the dispute can be solved. It is obvious that Beardsmore, while talking exclusively about the solution of disagreement in the first sense, thinks that his argument shows something about the possibility of solution in the second sense. As a result, we are almost brought to the point of saying that it is an empirical matter whether a dispute is logically capable of solution.

Talking of the agreement between a scientist and an anti-vivisectionist Beardsmore says: 'It is still possible that the dispute will be solved, if one of the disputants changes his views. It may, for instance, be that the scientist will just realise that he is wrong to attach an overriding importance to the pursuit of his researches.'[1]

Whether either can in fact convince the other must be irrelevant to the question of who, if anyone, is right. A plausible tongue is not the same as moral rectitude. If it is denied that the concepts of truth and knowledge have any application in the field of morality, it is necessary to be consistent. It will not be possible to talk of realising that one is 'wrong', as Beardsmore does, since there would be, *ex hypothesi*, no possibility of being 'right'. There would also

[1] Beardsmore, *Moral Reasoning*, p. 118.

be the not inconsiderable consequence that all discussion and argument about moral matters would become wholly pointless. If no-one is more likely to be right than anyone else, or rather if the very notion of 'being right' is inapplicable, the expression of moral opinions becomes merely the reporting of personal tastes and preferences (or of those of the community I belong to). There is nothing to argue about if I say I do not like bananas and you say you like tomatoes. However, the belief that moral discourse is subject to the standards of rationality seems to be built into the presuppositions of our language, and it is not surprising that Beardsmore lapses into using language which assumes the existence of some kind of objective standard in morality. It is perhaps significant that Kuhn also found it impossible to maintain a consistently relativist position in his treatment of science.

Freedom and commitment

One powerful motive for insisting that the notion of a commitment must be logically prior to that of a reason is that this seems to safeguard human freedom. It is often thought that any insistence that commitments must be justifiable suggests that men *have* to think in a certain way. On the other hand, if they have the power even to decide what will count as a reason, they seem to be in possession of very considerable personal freedom. They are not then forced into any commitment. Their freedom of choice is not restricted by the demands of rationality.

It is an undoubted fact that our personal decisions about what we shall commit ourselves to are *our* decisions. There must in this sense always be a subjective element in any commitment. No-one else can commit us to a religion, a morality or anything else of the kind. Someone who is forced by the state to pay lip-service to Communism can hardly be called a committed Communist. Hare makes a great deal of play in his moral theory with this feature of all commitments. He stresses that anyone faced with a moral problem 'knows that it is his own problem, and that nobody can answer it for him'.[1] He goes on to emphasise our freedom to form our own opinions about moral questions, and considers that in a moral context we are free 'in a much stronger sense than we are free to form our own opinions as to what the facts are'.[2]

This insistence on our freedom to form our own moral opinions is ambiguous. It may involve nothing more than a stress on the fact that we cannot shelve our responsibility for deciding which moral principles to adopt. We cannot blame our parents or our teachers for *our* moral principles. Even if we adopted them unthinkingly merely because we were taught them, we must be held responsible for them. An unthinking or irrational choice is still a choice. However much we may pretend otherwise, we are exercising our freedom when we make a moral judgment. No-one can force us to hold any particular moral belief. Even our acceptance of a moral position because of our respect for the authority of an individual or an institution must still be based on a decision *we* make. We would have decided to accept the pronouncements of the individual or the institution as being genuinely worthy of respect.

Hare means much more than this by his reference to moral freedom. He thinks that such freedom follows from the fact that 'there can be no logical deduction of moral judgments from statements of fact'. In other words, whatever the facts are, we are not forced to make any particular moral judgment. The snag with this is that we would not be *forced* to make the judgment even if it did logically follow from the facts. We are free to be illogical, just as we are free to be irrational. We are free to reject what is in fact conclusive

[1] Hare, *Freedom and Reason*, p. 1.
[2] *Ibid.* p. 2.

evidence for something, just as we are free to refuse to recognise the truth when it is presented to us. We are free to contradict ourselves and to be inconsistent. Presumably, if we are sane, we will do none of these things knowingly, but it by no means follows from the fact that something is the case that everyone will recognise it to be so. Indeed we are not forced to accept anything as a fact in the first place. This suggests that even if our moral opinions were thought to be of a similar type to our opinions about ordinary facts, there would still be plenty of room for the exercise of freedom. We would be free to decide what the facts are and we would be free to draw our own conclusions from them.

This certainly amounts in one sense to a 'freedom to form our own opinions' and perhaps provides all that is required for moral freedom, but Hare wants more than this. He considers that to hold that some moral principles might be reasonable or even right, while others were unreasonable or wrong, would itself be to restrict our freedom. Any restriction on what could count as a valid reason for a basic moral commitment (or 'decision of principle') would make us less free. As a result, according to Hare, moral freedom demands that the notion of a good (or a bad) reason for commitment is inappropriate, and that our choice of moral principles cannot be considered mistaken or wrong. I would then be free to decide which moral principles to adopt in a much stronger sense than I am free to be illogical. I would set my own standards and could not be judged by others.

We have seen that there is plenty of room for talk of 'moral freedom' without recourse to Hare's more extreme position. It is interesting, however, to see that his position is shared by others who have very different philosophic views. They, too, see the possibility of an objective justification for some basic commitment as a threat to freedom. MacIntyre produces an argument on these lines about religious commitment. He points out that if anyone who denied a Christian doctrine was immediately struck dead by a thunderbolt, England would soon be converted. He continues:

Since the Christian faith sees true religion only in a free decision made in faith and love, the religion would by this vindication be destroyed. For all possibility of free choice would have been done away. Any objective justification of belief would have the same effect. Less impressive than thunder-bolts, it would equally eliminate all possibility of a decision of faith. And with that, faith too would have been eliminated.[1]

There is clearly some point in all this from the religious point of view. The importance of freedom for faith might indeed provide one religious reason why it is not possible to *prove* the existence of God in the way one can prove a mathematical theorem (although even if it was possible, one would still be free to accept or reject the proof). One can, however, pursue this line of argument too far. Just because religion cannot be *proved* true, in a strong sense of 'prove', it does not follow that nothing can count for or against its truth. MacIntyre, however, wants to take the latter course. He says: 'To ask for a justification of religious belief as a whole is to ask for a something more ultimate than a fundamental conviction. If religious belief was not fundamental, it would not be religion.'

However, the fact that there may in principle be reasons for or against a commitment in no way need restrict one's freedom in deciding whether to make that commitment. The presence of reasons does not *force* us to adopt any particular position. No reason can have any influence until it is recognised by someone to be a reason. *If* there are reasons which have some kind of objective validity, their presence does nothing to reduce human freedom. Men would still be free to assess such reasons as they wish and to ignore or reject what are in fact perfectly good reasons for believing or doing something.

[1] MacIntyre (ed.), *Metaphysical Beliefs*, p. 209.

The possibility of intolerance

There is a related fallacy that any recognition of objective standards will inevitably lead to arrogance and intolerance, and eventually to the persecution of those who reject them. Nowell-Smith expresses what is at the back of many philosophers' minds when he maintains that the 'objectivist' is in an even worse position than the subjectivist in solving moral conflicts. He says of the objectivist:

He necessarily attributes his opponent's denial of the truth to wilful perversity, and, holding as he does that in spite of his denials his opponent must really see the truth all the time, he realises that what his opponent needs is not argument but castigation . . . It is no accident that religious persecutions are the monopoly of objective theorists.[1]

Nowell-Smith is writing about intuitionism in particular, but he might have levelled the same charges at any objectivist theory. If someone claims to be right and others do not agree with him, may not he be tempted to enforce what he believes to be right? The answer is of course that he may be. In the same way, a subjectivist may want to make everyone accept what he says, and he may resort to force precisely because he believes rational argument is impossible. Non-objectivist theories cannot distinguish between different methods of conversion. The objectivist, however, does believe that rational argument can at least in principle establish what is true; and there is no reason why someone who believes that basic disagreement *can* admit of solution firstly should arrogantly assume that he himself has a monopoly of truth, and secondly should then make others accept his views by force. The mere fact that a disagreement is capable of solution does not of itself suggest which side is right. When two sides flatly contradict each other, whether

[1] Nowell-Smith, *Ethics*, pp. 46–7.

in the fields of morality, religion or any other area, each will recognise (if they are objectivists) that at least one side must be mistaken. It could logically be *either*. To be consistent, therefore, an objectivist should recognise the possibility that he himself is mistaken. There need be no contradiction between strongly believing that one is right and yet realising that one could be wrong. Arrogance is not entailed by any objectivist theory. Certainly Nowell-Smith is wrong in thinking that any objectivist must consider that his opponent is disagreeing with him out of wilful perversity. An intuitionist theory which held that certain moral truths were self-evident might find itself in the position of having to say that everyone *must* see what is true. There are, however, other objectivist theories besides intuitionism, and it is no contradiction both to assert that truth is attainable in moral and religious matters and that it is often far from easy to arrive at it. It follows that sincere and reasonable men may find themselves disagreeing. The point, however, according to the objectivist is that they would be *disagreeing*. One would be asserting something which the other denied. They would be arguing about what was true.

Even if an objectivist were convinced that he was right and that others would benefit from his insight, it does not follow that he should impose his views on others by force. Indeed the toleration of views which are different from and even opposed to one's own is itself something which either admits of rational justification or does not. If it does, it is clear that the objectivist is right after all since there is at least one moral principle (that of toleration) which has objective validity. It follows that the objectivist would be mistaken not to adopt it. If it cannot be justified rationally, it is not very obvious what the critics of the objectivist are doing when they complain that his theory leads to intolerance. They may happen to think intolerance is a bad thing, but they cannot consistently say that anyone else should also think it is, without themselves adopting an objectivist position.

There is nothing intrinsic in non-objectivist views which promotes tolerance. Someone who thinks that although something is right or wrong for him or his society, he cannot speak for other people or other societies may *seem* to be very tolerant. He appears to be championing the right of everyone to make up his own mind. He cannot, however, uphold this as a *right*. The fact that he supports it does not on his view mean that others should. To put it round the other way, there can be no reason why he should be tolerant of opposing viewpoints. Talk of a 'reason' must suggest something which can be assessed by others and has some general validity, and he is denying the possibility of such a thing. Similarly, anyone who criticises any objectivist view in the name of freedom is immediately setting up at least one objective standard by which others may be judged, namely that of freedom.

7

Rationality

Determinism and conceptual relativism

We have been reasserting the possibility of giving rational justification for a commitment to a moral practice, a scientific theory, a religion, or any other 'form of life'. Relativists do not agree amongst themselves what kind of commitment could count as ultimate and unjustifiable. Commitments to Roman Catholicism, Christianity, and religion have all been held to set the standards of rationality in the appropriate area. Western science, physics, and particular scientific theories have each been mentioned as comprising self-contained conceptual systems.

However confusing the details of these theories may be, the basic claims are clear enough. It is held that there are separate, although possibly overlapping, systems of thought, which can be judged only by the standards they themselves create. Either one is an adherent of a system and grasps its concepts or one is outside and as a result must find it incomprehensible. One's commitment determines what is a reason, and one cannot give reasons for the commitment. Beliefs about what is the case can form no basis for this kind of commitment, since the commitment itself determines what is to count as a fact, or as 'reality'. Any decision to join or opt out of a 'system' or 'form of life' must be outside the scope of reason.

When truth is divided into watertight compartments, so that what is true for one group may not be true for another, and may not even be intelligible to them, the notion of an all-embracing rationality must be completely abandoned. If I am barred from thinking of what is true as a first step towards deciding what to commit myself to, there will be no firm basis for making the commitment. It will either be totally arbitrary, or caused. The connection between commitment and propositional belief, which I have previously insisted upon, must be ruled out by conceptual relativism, for the simple reason that what will count as a proposition will depend on the system of which it is a part. Propositional belief already presupposes a system, according to the conceptual relativist. It cannot therefore be used to justify one (except, possibly, as a part of a wider whole).

The notion of an ultimate arbitrary commitment from which everything springs is in many ways an unsatisfactory one, although popular in some quarters. Some of those who have faced the problems which result from versions of conceptual relativism have not surprisingly felt the need to show that explanations for the ultimate commitments which people make individually or collectively are still available. We have seen how Kuhn thought the explanation of scientific progress 'must, in the final analysis, be psychological or sociological'.[1] Whether others putting forward similar views have realised it or not, the undermining of the role of reason and the emphasis that truth is relative to systems has paved the way to this conclusion. If reasons cannot be given to justify men committing themselves to one system rather than another, it is a fairly obvious step to say that we must look for causes to explain the existence of different 'systems' or forms of life. If the holding of concepts is essentially a social matter, then the sociologists can provide causal explanations as to why particular communities should be as they are. The problem why an individual stays in or out of a particular community, when there can be no good reason for his leaving or joining, can be passed over to the psychologist. Between them, the two specialists would seem to be able to answer all the questions which can be intelligibly asked about

[1] Kuhn, 'Reflections on my Critics', p. 21.

the situation. All that we can do is to look for causes why things are as they are.

Even though conceptual relativism seems to lead to deterministic explanations, there does remain the question whether it should in fact do so. The explanations which sociologists and psychologists give can no more be regarded as *true* by conceptual relativists than the beliefs of the system under scrutiny. The explanations must themselves only be valid within sociology or psychology. Even this is probably too large a claim. Since sociologists or psychologists may well fundamentally disagree amongst themselves about what counts as an adequate explanation in their discipline, the various explanations may well have only to be regarded as valid within a particular school of sociologists or psychologists.

The very considerations which apparently make people turn to psychology and sociology for enlightenment would also ensure that these disciplines could give no help in explaining why men have certain commitments. The commitments just exist and some men happen to be committed to the standards of psychology or of sociology. Once it is denied that there can be any standards which are valid for everyone, it is open to anyone to reject these disciplines, just as others have rejected other commitments. If it is argued that their explanations fit the facts as no others do, that they provide the possibility of making successful predictions and so on, the conceptual relativist can give the familiar reply that all this merely begs the question. Why, he might say, should *these* be counted as relevant facts, or why should such-and-such a prediction be thought to be successful? The answer he would give is that we think like this as a result of our prior commitment to psychology or sociology (or at least to the procedures of modern science of which they form a part). The disciplines themselves decide what is relevant, and even what is to count as a fact. Kuhn's faith in them is merely evidence of his own commitment to science as it is understood in the contemporary Western world. If conceptual relativism were correct, one could dismiss psychology and sociology out of hand, for no scientific explanations could be regarded as having objective validity.

But paradoxically a belief in determinism may itself lead to conceptual relativism. If we hold that all our beliefs and commitments are causally explicable, rationality and questions of truth and falsity become irrelevant. In these circumstances the commitment of a Marxist or a Christian cannot be affected by reason. He is what he is because of his upbringing, his environment, his genetic make-up or whatever other causal explanation may be given. The fact that one set of beliefs might be true and another false could not possibly affect him. He will only take to be true what he is caused to believe and will only think something a good reason if he is caused to. Determinism makes all disagreement a matter for causal explanation, and as a result makes it impossible in principle to conceive of the rational solution of any disagreement. Whether the two parties to a dispute eventually agree is determined by the causal influences at work. Reason can have no independent role, according to determinism, because it must itself be merely the product of a chain of causes. Indeed because *all* reasoning must for a determinist be caused, this raises difficulties about his belief in determinism. As has often been pointed out, it seems to be self-defeating to maintain that determinism is true, since one's belief in determinism could also be causally explained. Determinism does not deny the possibility of objective truth. It is just that what is actually true, as opposed to what we are caused to believe is true, becomes an impossible goal.

This is a highly controversial argument, but I cannot pursue it far here. It has been challenged, for example, by A. Grünbaum:

The causal generation of a belief in no way detracts from its veridicality. In fact, if a given belief were not produced in us by definite causes, we should have no reason to accept that belief as a correct description of the world, rather than some other belief arbitrarily selected.[1]

This last sentence is revealing, as it implicitly accepts that the only alternative to a caused belief is one *arbitrarily* chosen. It is thus merely an assertion that causal explanation must be the only possible form of explanation, and that one cannot have reasons unless they are causes. This position is not self-evident and requires argument. Why, for instance, should an arbitrary choice itself not be caused? A computer can be programmed to make random selections.

Grünbaum tries to retain a contrast between rational and irrational beliefs by distinguishing between different types of causes:

A warrantedly held belief, which has the presumption of being true, is one to which a person gave assent in response to awareness of supporting evidence. Assent in the face of awareness of a *lack* of supporting evidence is irrational, although there are indeed psychological causes in such cases for giving assent.

He goes on to contrast the man who assents to a belief because it is wish-fulfilling, and the man who accepts the same conclusion 'in response to his recognition of the existence of strong supporting evidence'. This raises the question of what can count as strong supporting evidence in a determinist system. It may be possible to distinguish the rational belief from the irrational one, even though both are caused, if we have a prior standard of rationality. If we know what good evidence is, then a belief based on it can be seen to be rational. The snag is that, if determinism is correct, our beliefs about what constitutes good evidence, and even of what evidence is relevant, are themselves caused. We then cannot know whether we think something good

[1] Grünbaum, 'Free Will and Laws of Human Behaviour', *American Philosophical Quarterly*, October 1971, p. 309.

evidence because it is, or because of something quite extraneous. We are in no position to distinguish finally between a rational belief and an irrational one. We can only have beliefs about the matter which themselves may be vitiated by wish-fulfilment or some such outside factor.

How might determinism lead to conceptual relativism? When everyone by and large believes the same things, the determinist is in no great difficulties, despite his emphasis on the causes of belief rather than reasons. Things get awkward for him if there is considerable disagreement. People's natural response in such a situation is to ask 'which is true?' or 'who is right?' but a determinist must hold that those who argue are merely suffering an illusion when they think they are rationally settling these questions. What each person decides, or what they collectively decide, can be wholly explained by reference to the causal forces at work. It can thus become tempting for the determinist to say that there is no such thing as truth, and that it is causally explicable that different people happen to be committed to different beliefs. As a result, all possibility of justification has to be ruled out, since all attempts at justification are themselves merely the products of a causal chain. It is only a small step from this to classifying people in groups and pointing out the differences in ways of thought which exist between the various groups. A determinist could maintain that there were causes for the differences. There could be no notion that the various groups were attempting to interpret the same reality, since it would be impossible in principle to give any independent characterisation of reality which was not itself caused. 'Reality' would thus vary according to how the groups viewed it with their various conceptual systems, and all the consequences of conceptual relativism would immediately appear.

Not all determinists will be attracted by this line of argument, and may, for instance, challenge the rigid distinction I have assumed between reasons and causes. Determinism, however, would have to give a causal explanation of why someone counted one thing a good reason, another a bad reason, and something else no reason at all. A person's holding of a reason merely becomes a link in the causal chain. Questions of truth and falsity become irrelevant in these circumstances, and the whole emphasis shifts from the question what is true to the question why a man believes this or that to be true.

Even when apparent experts agree, determinists would no doubt hold that a sociological explanation was forthcoming. Explanations can be given, too, of why people may think differently, but there is no possibility of showing that anyone is mistaken in thinking as he does. If a large group agree in thinking that, for instance, the procedures of Western science, including a commitment to determinism, provide the means for establishing what is true, the strict determinist must hold that this is merely an interesting fact about them, itself susceptible to scientific investigation. They cannot be judged finally correct or mistaken in what they believe, although we may ourselves agree or disagree with them. This means that the determinist cannot consistently hold that his own commitment to determinism can be justified. It is explicable causally, and is no better or worse than, say, a commitment to the beliefs and practices of Voodoo.

By ruling out the possibility that any purported rational justification and criticism could ever be known to have any general validity, determinism encourages the belief that everyone ultimately makes a caused commitment to a whole system of thought. Such systems may themselves include ideas about what is true, but these must inevitably be relative to the system. There is no way left of adjudicating between systems and establishing the truth by any uncaused process of reason.

Determinism joins forces with conceptual relativism in

focussing all our attention on the fact of our belief rather than its content. Why people believe something is a totally different question from the validity of what is believed. The latter depends on whether their beliefs reflect what really is the case, and reality can in no way be dependent on their beliefs. By attacking the possibility of uncaused rationality determinism makes conceptual relativism more attractive. It does not actually *entail* conceptual relativism, which clearly involves very distinctive views about the relationship between concepts and societies. In the same way, conceptual relativism does not *entail* determinism (indeed, it actually undermines it, as we saw). However determinism is certainly in its turn made superficially more attractive, when the only alternative is to accept the impossibility of giving any explanation for differences of belief between various communities.

Bartley and the possibility of rationality

It is at this point that someone may point out that it is all very well pleading the case for a rationality which is all-embracing and not relative to a particular form of life. He may wish to know why he should be rational anyway, and why anyone should think that it matters whether we have good reasons for our belief or are prepared to listen to argument. He might insist that this too was in the end a matter of individual commitment. If he does not feel like being rational, is he in any worse position than someone who does? W. W. Bartley poses the problem as follows:

Obviously, a man cannot, without arguing in a circle, justify the rationality of his standard of rationality by appealing to that standard. Yet, if he holds certain beliefs – for example the standard itself – to be immune from the demand for rational justification and from the question 'How do you know?' he can be said to hold them irrationally or dogmatically.

And, so it is claimed, arguments among men about the radically different beliefs they hold in this way is pointless.[1]

The problem of justifying any commitments apparently comes down in the end to the problem of whether commitment to rationality itself can be justified. Bartley presents us with the problem that rationalists may be as irrational as those who glory in the fact that ultimate commitments must be made arbitrarily, and that they too may be making an arbitrary commitment. He quotes Ayer's attempt to deal with the difficulty. Ayer says of scientific method: 'It could be irrational only if there were a standard of rationality which it failed to meet: whereas in fact it goes to set the standard: arguments are judged to be rational or irrational by reference to it.'[2] As Bartley points out[3] Ayer's argument begs the whole question whether his position is the correct one. It is all very well for Ayer to say that what he is committed to sets the standard. Those who would disagree with him (for example, believers in oracles) would remain unconvinced. They are equally able to say that *their* position sets the standard. Ayer is in fact laying down by definition what is going to count as a rational standard, and it is clearly open to others to refuse to accept such a definition.

Any attempt to justify rationality must avoid the charge of merely laying something down by definition, and must also avoid any suspicion of invoking an arbitrary commitment. The trouble is that any justification which does more than say what is to be deemed rational must give reasons for rationality which are themselves subject to rational scrutiny. The circularity involved in this latter exercise seems inherent in any justification of rationality. It seems as if it is logically impossible to justify being rational. There is only a short step from this admission to the view that the rational man

[1] Bartley, *The Retreat to Commitment*, p. 91.
[2] Ayer, *The Problem of Knowledge*, p. 75.
[3] Bartley, *The Retreat to Commitment*, p. 129.

does himself make a non-rational commitment, and that he is in no position to criticise anyone else who makes any other kind of arbitrary commitment.

Bartley squarely faces this problem and produces his own answer to it. He advocates what he calls 'comprehensively critical rationalism'. This is basically an openness of mind which involves a readiness to expose everything, including one's rationality, to criticism. He says: 'If rationality lies in criticism, and if one can subject everything to criticism and continued test, including the rationalist way of life itself, then rationality is unlimited.'[1]

At no stage is one involved in an arbitrary commitment which cannot itself be examined. The pursuit of rationality can thus be distinguished from say, an ultimate, unjustifiable commitment to a religion, and the rationalist cannot be said to be in the same position as those he might wish to criticise. Bartley's position has itself been subjected to critical scrutiny[2] and indeed seems to have some curious consequences. Not least amongst them is the fact that if one gave up one's 'comprehensively critical rationalism', because one was persuaded by some adverse criticism of it, this would seem to be a vindication of the doctrine. If one accepts that it can be shown to be false, this thereby seems to exhibit its truth. On the other hand, if one refuses to accept that it could be shown to be false by criticism, it would seem that this would itself be irrational according to the doctrine. Yet if one already has good grounds for believing it to be true, it is surely not irrational to refuse to give serious consideration to all adverse criticism.

Once it is realised that not all criticism will necessarily be relevant, a theory of rationality which emphasises the importance of criticism begins to look as if it is begging some important questions. What, for instance, is to count as

[1] Bartley, *The Retreat to Commitment*, p. 147.
[2] See articles by J. W. N. Watkins and others in *Philosophy*, January 1971.

criticism in the first place? Much of the impetus towards relativism comes from the fact that it seems impossible to get agreed standards. What one man thinks is a crucial test for a theory, may be thought relevant but not crucial by another, and irrelevant by a third. My refusal to give up a view in face of severe criticism may prove to my critics that it is held irrationally. I may, however, feel that their attempted criticism totally misses the mark, and that their arguments do not warrant the title of 'criticism'. To uphold willingness to face criticism as the criterion of rationality will not solve this particular confrontation. Even if their criticism is apparently to the point, it by no means follows that I should accept it and give up or modify my views. If my opponents are merely offering destructive criticism and no better alternative to my view is available, it might be more rational to hold on to it than to hold no view at all. As the history of science suggests, there is place for some stubbornness in holding to theories even when the experimental evidence seems to go against them. When a theory clashes with experimental findings, it is sometimes as possible that the experiments were wrong as that the theory is false.

Although there is some sense in this line of argument, it could if pressed lead us in science to Kuhn's brand of relativism where what we are willing to count as a fact depends on which scientific paradigm we owe allegiance to. This is very significant, since it demonstrates that Bartley has in no way met the basic problems of rationality. He has assumed that rationality is possible and there is one set of standards to which everyone should appeal. One response he could and probably would make, is that his theory demands that one's critical standards themselves should be subject to criticism. Consequently, if there is disagreement about which critical standards to adopt, then the various positions which give rise to the standards must themselves be scrutinised. This is merely to move the problem one stage back. There is no guarantee that common ground can be found in scrutinising the various critical standards. The choice seems to lie between the possibility of an infinite regress and accepting that reference to criticism does nothing to show that rational criticism is more than an illusion.

Anything can be criticised, but it is another matter whether the criticisms are valid. This brings us back to the problem whether there can be objective standards of criticism. Anyone who asks 'why be rational?', by asking for reasons, assumes that there are reasons, and that rationality is in principle possible. This does not mean the question is a stupid one. The questioner may, for example, be asking why he should use argument rather than force. The point is, though, that he is asking for reasons and thus has already involved himself in the whole process of rationality. Even if he decides it is right to use force, he is not using it as an alternative to rationality. Reasoning has itself led him to this conclusion.

The search for a justification of rationality is what led Bartley to his position. He saw that talk of commitment to rationality involved one in the admission that the commitment was arbitrary, and that, as he puts it, 'rationality is so limited that *everyone* has to make a dogmatic, irrational commitment'.[1] There must, however, be something very wrong with the notion of a *justification* of rationality, because clearly it is itself a concept from *within* rationality. Anyone who wants such a justification wants to stand outside the framework of rationality while remaining inside, and this is obviously incoherent. Bartley's own words point to the oddity of his concern. If rationality is limited, it is wrong to think that a commitment made outside its scope is *irrational*. It could not be at variance with what is rational, when rationality does not extend that far. Just because it is non-rational does not mean that it is positively irrational. Once

[1] Bartley, *The Retreat to Commitment*, p. 90.

again Bartley is assuming the possibility of rationality and feels that it is wrong that anything should fall outside its scope. Anything which is not in accordance with rationality must, he assumes, be opposed to it and thus be irrational. He takes it for granted that one must be able to justify a position, but this could clearly only be so if it is logically possible that a justification be forthcoming. If it is not, there can be no shame in not being able to give one.

Bartley ignores the most basic question of all, namely whether rationality is possible in the first place. As we have seen in earlier chapters, some would protect their own personal commitments from criticism by denying that the commitments were either reasonable or unreasonable. Similarly those who see that a certain amount of argument and justification is possible given certain presuppositions, would stress the importance of communities with their own conceptual systems which cannot be scrutinised rationally from outside. Both groups would be judged irrational according to Bartley's account of rationality, and yet this is obviously far too quick a way of dealing with basic challenges to the possibility of an all-embracing rationality. When somebody is sceptical about rationality, it is merely to beg the question to tell him why he is being irrational.

The preconditions of language

Strictly speaking, only the subjectivist completely denies the possibility of rationality. Very few people wish to join Protagoras and hold a consistently subjectivist position for all classes of statements. Nevertheless, in so far as someone is a subjectivist, he is challenging the basis of rationality. This is self-evidently the case if he denies that his beliefs or commitments are a matter of reason at all. Even if he maintains that he has reasons, but that he is free to decide what he will count as a reason and his reasons are not necessarily valid for anyone else, this amounts to a refusal to admit the possibility of rationality. If irrationality is in principle impossible, rationality must be an illusion.

The conceptual relativist can to a certain extent accept this risk. He would emphasise that what counted as a good reason for belief would depend on the system or form of life. A Christian could be judged irrational by the standards of his fellow Christians but Christianity itself could not be judged an irrational system of belief. Rationality, like truth, would be compartmentalised. This would be no accident since the two concepts are inextricably entwined. If what is true varies from system to system what counts as a reason for belief must also vary. It may be rational to believe in God if one is a Christian and irrational if one is a Marxist. All this allows some limited scope for the concepts of rationality and irrationality, but the conceptual relativist is in precisely the same position as the subjectivist when it comes to questions concerning commitment to one system rather than another. He can allow no rational answer to questions such as 'Why be a Christian?' or 'Why practise Western science?'

It is curious that the challenges of subjectivism and relativism seem only to be met with difficulty. The possibility of rationality is such a basic assumption that anyone who denies it seems to leave rationalists with little to say. However, the very idea of a 'rationalist' in the sense of someone who believes in and is committed to rationality is extremely odd. Rationality cannot be an optional extra, if it is possible at all. Either it is at root an illusion, and everyone ultimately has to make a non-rational commitment, or each person's commitment can be rationally scrutinised. I cannot myself decide whether I am subject to the demands of rationality, in the way that I can decide to be a Conservative or a Socialist. I may decide to ignore the constraints of rationality, but if there is such a thing, I am thereby being irrational. We cannot make a commitment to rationality.

Either there is nothing to be committed to, or the notion of committing oneself is inappropriate. We cannot put ourselves beyond the standards of rationality, if an all-embracing rationality is possible, but this claim will not satisfy those who are worried precisely about whether it is possible. What difference does talk about rationality make in a situation of basic disagreement between two opposing views, where it seems impossible to settle the matter by agreement or by appeal to facts? Questions about justification and reasonableness seem unreal when the atheist and the Christian for example, reach the end of an argument in total disagreement. This, of course, is where the conceptual relativist begins to make his case and it is precisely when he also overplays his hand. As we have seen, conceptual relativism results in the compartmentalisation of language and understanding. It leads to the impossibility of expressing the disagreement in terms both sides could understand. It tries to explain the disagreement by showing that there is no disagreement, because neither side can contradict the other. Each side is operating with different concepts, it holds, and they must to a large extent be talking about different things. They live in 'different worlds'.

If we wish to maintain that *disagreement* on fundamental issues is possible, that there is room for argument and discussion on such matters, and that there can be reasons for and against adopting any view, then it is inevitable that we turn again to the concept of truth. What people disagree about is what is true, and not merely what is true for them. If there is no such thing as truth in a certain area people cannot disagree. Indeed they cannot even begin to communicate with each other. Communication within a form of life was judged possible because there was an agreed standard of truth. This emphasis on human agreement must be misguided. People who disagree (often at a fundamental level) can talk to each other. It is crucial to realise that what people agree about and what is true are very different and yet closely linked. If a belief is false, the fact that many people hold it does not make it any less false. Nevertheless the motive force behind argument and the desire for agreement is normally the search for truth. One would have to be very cynical to hold that it does not matter what people believe as long as they agree, and it would be an impossible policy to carry out oneself. When I know that something is not true, or have no grounds for thinking that it is, I cannot, except possibly in extreme instances of self-deception, be said to believe it.

If language can be used as a means of communication (and the writing of this sentence assumes that this is so), certain presuppositions must be built into it. Human agreement on particular issues is not one of them. It is purely contingent whether what people happen to believe is true. What is of supreme importance is that there is some notion of truth as such in human language. This is the cement which binds language together and stops it being fragmented into self-contained compartments, such as religious language. It is this which enables people of different views to understand each other, and allows the sentences of one language to be translated into those of another. An essential function of language, in other words, is to communicate truth, or at least purported truths. Language cannot, of course, be confined to this simple statement-making role, but this is its central purpose. When I say something to you, I normally intend that you should understand me to be making a claim about what is or is not the case. If I say that it is raining you can then look out of the window and then either agree or disagree. This is the simplest kind of case, and obviously it is more complicated to say that God exists. Nevertheless the point is that even there you are free to agree *or disagree*. You can understand and reject what I say, because you too can examine what you think is the case, and form your own conclusions.

It follows that if we are not merely suffering the illusion

that we can understand those we disagree with, language must be understood to be about one world, where certain states of affairs hold. Language and the world cannot be totally disconnected, since a major purpose of the former is to describe the latter. The relationship between them, however, must not be made to appear closer than it is. Different languages such as French, English, Swedish or any other, or even different types of language, such as scientific language and religious language, do not refer to a different world. They all refer in their different ways to the same world, and at times they may misdescribe it. This must be so whenever there is a conflict about what is the case, since in any disagreement both sides cannot be equally right. For instance it cannot both be raining and not raining, and the world cannot both be God's creation and the result of a totally random process of evolution. The inability of one side to convince the other does not mean that notions of truth and falsity are inappropriate. It is because it is possible to distinguish in principle between what the world is like and what we say it is like that disagreement is possible. Those who disagree are talking about the same things, even if they are making totally different claims about them. Anyone who wishes to deny this has to deny that disagreement is possible.

The concept of truth does not merely underpin those of belief and disagreement. Because a main function of language is to talk about and communicate what is the case, the absence of any distinction between truth and falsity (i.e. between what is and is not so) will destroy language. Anything could then be said with impunity, and nothing could be ruled out as inappropriate. This would render it pointless to say anything, since there would be no difference in practice between assertion and denial. It would be impossible ever to teach a language. If there was no chance of using it incorrectly it would be impossible to pass on the correct application of words and sentences, since *ex hypothesi* there would be no such thing. Nor could we ever be sure that we were using words in the same way. As a result, what you meant by 'It is raining' may be very different from what I meant. Since the words could be used to cover any situation from sunshine to the cat having its dinner, they will communicate nothing to me.

Plato faced a similar problem when in the *Theaetetus* he examined the implications of Protagoras' subjectivism. He thought that if Protagoras was right in maintaining that every man was correct in what he perceived, and if language was about the world, Protagoras' position entailed Heraclitus' view that the world was in a constant state of flux. Different men would report different perceptions and therefore the world *was* different for each of them, and must be continually changing.[1] It is interesting, however, that Plato only thought this because of his own objectivist assumption that there was one world even if *it* was the subject of change. If he had recognised the possibility that different men lived in different worlds, he need not have brought in Heraclitus' views, although he would have had to recognise that individuals could not communicate with each other and language would be impossible, because they would forever be talking about different things. As it was, the introduction of Heraclitus brought Plato to the same conclusion. He holds that even in one world constant change undermines language, since it leaves words with no fixed reference. Whiteness, for example, would change instantly into another colour. As a result Socrates asks 'can we ever give it the name of any colour and be sure that ˌwe are naming it rightly?' If things altered quickly, the words which apply to them would be unable to retain their meaning. Indeed, if we take Heraclitus' thought to its logical conclusion, and assume that things not only constantly change their characteristics but change in their basic nature or 'substance', it would be impossible for words

[1] Plato, *Theaetetus*, 182 D.

ever to pick out anything in the world. No sooner than one
had identified a dog, than 'it' would have changed into a
horse, then a tree, then a stone and so on, so that identifica-
tion and re-identification would be ruled out. Once again
communication would be rendered impossible.

Language must be understood to be about one world open
to public inspection, Plato's criticism of Protagoras and
Heraclitus also makes it clear that it is a precondition of
language that the world has a certain stability. There is in
fact no practical difference between there being a world in
which things are constantly changing and are not the same
for everyone, and there being many different worlds. We
must have the assurance that when we pick things out and
draw other people's attention to them, they too can identify
what we are referring to, and agree or disagree with what we
say.

The conceptual relativist could agree with this latter point
and insist that communication is in fact limited. We do not
all share the same language, it might be argued, and there is
a real 'intelligibility gap' between those who live in different
worlds because they participate in different forms of life.
We have already seen the insuperable difficulties against
deciding what is to count as a form of life, and once it is
agreed that forms of life can overlap, all point in talking about
them seems to disappear. Whatever the other drawbacks
of the theory, it runs into the same problem as any brand of
relativism. In saying that truth is an internal matter for the
different forms of life, and that people in effect live in different worlds, the conceptual relativist seems to be making
assertions about what is the case. He is himself making
claims about what is objectively true. In talking about forms
of life, he seems himself to be stepping outside them. It is of
course open to him to say that his words are only true for the
form of life in which he is participating. It is part of the
general incoherence of the position that others would not

even begin to know whether they were members of the same form of life or not. Presumably if they understand what he says, they must be.

If his view of truth is correct, there is no room for any disagreement, since only those who agreed with it could grasp what was being said. This is, to say the least, an odd position for someone putting forward a serious philosophical view. Even to talk of the possibility of its being correct must be wrong. It is just part of the fabric of a particular form of life, and as such would have only a sociological interest. In fact, however, those philosophers who have preached versions of conceptual relativism have used language normally, and have not put forward their views as if they only applied to a limited range of people. Even the relativist, if he uses language at all, has eventually to say something which purports to be *true*.

Understanding and translation

Quine, in a famous example, points to a basic indeterminacy in translation which seems to exist when a linguist tries to translate a hitherto unknown language. He envisages a rabbit scurrying by, a native saying 'Gavagai' and the linguist noting down 'Rabbit' (or 'Lo, a rabbit'). Quine asks about 'gavagai':

Who knows but what the objects to which this term applies are not rabbits after all, but mere stages, or brief temporal segments, of rabbits. In either event, the stimulus situations that prompt assent to 'Gavagai' would be the same as for 'Rabbit'. Or perhaps the objects to which 'gavagai' applies are all and sundry undetached parts of rabbits; again the stimulus meaning would register no difference.[1]

It would be impossible ever to decide what was really meant, because, as Quine puts it, 'a whole rabbit is present when and only when an undetached part of a rabbit is

[1] Quine, *Word and Object*, p. 51.

present; also, when and only when a temporal stage of a rabbit is present'.[1] Similarly, the native could be talking of 'rabbithood'. The native's use of 'Gavagai' and our use of 'Rabbit' would thus always coincide, even though theoretically we may not conceive what we are talking about in the same way. However, exactly the same set of circumstances would always make our statement, 'There's a rabbit' and the native's 'Gavagai' true, and so there is no bar to our understanding him or his understanding us. We know what circumstances hold when he says 'Gavagai', and he could learn what circumstances hold when we say 'Rabbit'. (Quine allows that we are each subject to the same visual stimulation.) The alleged indeterminacy of translation is thus irrelevant to whether it is logically possible to get to grips with another society's conception of the world. Difficulties arising from different methods of individuation do not necessarily undermine the notion of objectivity.

Two questions must be kept separate. First, might a society be said to have such basically different conceptions of the way things are that they could be said to live in different worlds? This is relativism. Entirely distinct from this is the problem whether, even given the same world, and the same perceptions of it, there may in different societies be a consistent and subtle difference in methods of individuating objects. In this latter case, as we have seen, what is true is the same for both groups of people. What is there is independent of their beliefs about it. As a result, once we have learnt each other's language, we are in a position to contradict each other. When a shadow passes quickly in front of us in poor light, a native might say 'Gavagai'. If we had seen that it was definitely not a rabbit, although it could have been, we would be in a position to say that he was mistaken. Similarly, there might be occasions when the native could legitimately contradict our shout of 'Rabbit!'

[1] Quine, *Ontological Relativity*, p. 30.

The apparent inscrutability of reference shown by Quine's example is difficult precisely because the native and the linguist are always referring to the same section of the same world, and it seems unlikely that their different principles of individuation can ever be discovered. For this very reason it is a factor of little importance in communication. Kuhn, however, seizes on the example and extends it by supposing that in the native's community, 'rabbits change colour, length of hair, characteristic gait, and so on during the rainy season, and that their appearance then elicits the term "Bavagai"'. He then asks:

> Should 'Bavagai' be translated 'wet rabbit', 'shaggy rabbit', 'limping rabbit', all of these together, or should the linguist conclude that the native community has not recognised that 'Bavagai' and 'Gavagai' refer to the same animal? Evidence relevant to a choice among these alternatives will emerge from further investigation, and the result will be a reasonable analytic hypothesis with implications for the translation of other terms as well.[1]

Kuhn goes on to emphasise that it would only be a hypothesis since none of the proposed alternatives need be right. This is to suggest that a translator of an unknown language will certainly find it difficult narrowing down the possible meanings of a word. In Kuhn's example, he will have to find out the reactions of a native to wet rabbits which are not shaggy and do not limp, shaggy rabbits which are not wet and so on. This does not mean that an adequate translation is in principle impossible. As long as we assume that the native and we see the same world in the same way, it should be comparatively straightforward to discover what he says in specified situations. Difficulties arise only when it is suggested that a native sees things so differently from us that he and we can in no sense be said to be living in the same world or reacting to the same situation. What we see as a wet, shaggy, limping rabbit may not be distinguished at all

[1] Kuhn, 'Reflections on my Critics', p. 268.

from its background by the native. Much of what Kuhn says about the incommensurability of theories suggests that he might be tempted to take this more radical line, but this is to remove the whole basis for any translation whatever. Kuhn's talk of having an analytic hypothesis, which, presumably, might be mistaken, tends to obscure this point. Unless we assume that the native and we are living in the same world, there is no way of even beginning a translation. The native's words may divide up the world differently from ours, but the point is that his words must pick out differences which we too can notice. If his words are understood to be about a world which is in principle closed to our inspection because it is not objective but is dependent on his beliefs, the possibility of understanding becomes a mirage.

In such circumstances, we would have no guarantee that any attempt at translation could succeed, and indeed we would have no idea of what would constitute success. Even when we apparently understood the natives, we could well be talking at complete cross-purposes. If their world and ours are each self-contained, guesses at correspondence between the two must be made without any basis at all. Even if our worlds apparently overlapped to some extent, there would be no criteria to which we could appeal to find out how far in fact they corresponded. This is not just to challenge the possibility of translation. It is to question the possibility of ever learning another language such as that of the native. Without the assumption of one objective world, we cannot even begin to understand the circumstances in which a member of another community utters a sentence or a word. Any hypothesis about what he might be talking about must depend on the assumption that we have access to the same objects.

We have been talking of everyday language, but what we are saying has equal relevance to the very possibility of understanding, and if necessary translating, another man's use of religious, moral or scientific language. He might not be talking about 'things' which we can see or touch, but he must not be understood to be making claims about a world the existence of which depends in some way on a prior commitment. His claims must be judged by external criteria of truth and falsity. Otherwise, as we have seen, those who do not share his commitment can never hope to understand him. A Christian must not be thought to live in a different world from the non-Christian. The holder of one scientific theory must not be conceived of as living in a different world from the holder of another. The fact that people hold different beliefs does not mean that the beliefs are about different things. The beliefs are all about the same world, but some of them are *false*.

The same argument applies to holders of different moral beliefs. If they disagree about the significance to be given to certain facts, it is too easy to think of them as just living with different moralities, seeing things differently, and thus in a sense living in different worlds. This would make mutual understanding and even the formulation of disagreement impossible in moral matters which nevertheless have all the appearance of being highly controversial. The comparison of different moral outlooks would be in principle impossible.

In fact, the relativist view of 'different worlds' with the ensuing impossibility of translation from the terms of one world to those of another, poses a fundamental threat to all intellectual disciplines which depend on a comparison of opposing viewpoints, and a detached appraisal of differing systems of thought. If understanding and commitment go hand in hand, anthropology and sociology are certainly threatened. In addition, the history of science and of religion become in principle impossible. It is ironic that the notion of the incommensurability of scientific theories is given support by proponents such as Kuhn and Feyerabend with the use of examples from the history of science. The very same notion undermines the whole basis of the history of science. If translation between the terms of a theory which has been superseded and those of the present day is in principle totally impossible, we may well wonder how it is possible ever to have any idea that we have achieved an adequate understanding of all the old theory. *Ex hypothesi*, we can only understand it on its terms, and it is hard to see how in principle we could begin to get to grips with them.

It is crucial to distinguish two possible positions. We may accept that different communities have different beliefs and say different things about the same world. It does not follow from this that each language will have an exact equivalent for words to be found in another, any more than different scientific theories may use terms in an exactly similar way. As a result there may be at times some difficulty in providing a satisfactory translation. What, for instance is the English equivalent of the German *Angst* or the Greek *agapē*? The interesting thing about these cases is that an Englishman can see the inadequacy of any one English word as a translation of these. He can see the distinctions the words are making, and express them in English, even though he can use no single English word to do the job. The same truth conditions exist for statements in English and, say, German. A second position is the logical thesis about 'different worlds', which would forever lock up different languages, and even different uses of the same language, in self-contained compartments. This second position is that of the relativist.

It is a favourite ploy to slide from one position to another. Most relativists will only admit that it is very difficult to translate adequately, and in fact use this difficulty to support their belief in relativism. B. L. Whorf, whose linguistic studies made him aware of the different ways language could divide up the world, actually embraces the term 'relativist'. He talks of a 'new principle of relativity which holds that all observers are not led by the same physical evidence to the same picture of the universe, unless their linguistic backgrounds are similar, or can in some way be calibrated'.

This suggests that people from one linguistic background may find it impossible to understand those whose background is very different. Whorf enlarges on this point when he says:

When Semitic, Chinese, Tibetan or African languages are contrasted with our own, the divergence in analysis of the world becomes more apparent: and when we bring in the native language of the Americas, whose speech communities for many millenniums have gone their ways independently of each other and of the Old World, the fact that languages dissect nature in many different ways becomes patent. The relativity of all conceptual systems, ours included, and their dependence upon language stand revealed.[1]

This looks like an unqualified acceptance of conceptual relativism, but an examination of Whorf's examples show that he is concerned with the different ways language classify things in the *same* world. Thus the language of the Hopi Indians classifies brief events (such as lightning, wave or flame) as verbs, while Whorf says that in Nootka (a language of Vancouver Island) all words seem to us to be verbs. He reports that 'a house occurs' or 'it houses' is its way of saying 'house'. He continues:

Hopi has one noun that covers every thing or being that flies, with the exception of birds . . . The Hopi actually call insect, airplane and aviator all by the same word, and feel no difficulty about it . . . This class seems to us too large and inclusive, but so would our class 'snow' to an Eskimo.[2]

There are clearly many ways of classifying and grouping together objects and events in the world. The fact that different languages may do it differently does not of itself suggest that they are referring to different states of affairs or 'different worlds'. Other languages can make distinctions

[1] Whorf, *Language, Thought and Reality* (ed. J. Carroll), p. 214.
[2] *Ibid*, p. 216.

which ours ignores, or not notice differences we think crucial. The important point is that we can notice the different kinds of snow the Eskimo talks about, and presumably the Hopi could be brought to see the differences between various kinds of things which fly. Whether we use one word or six for snow or things which fly, the same truth conditions hold. The differences are not relative to a conceptual system, even if one such system draws attention to them and another ignores them. When there is no snow, the Eskimo is just as wrong if he uses any of his words as he would be if we used our one. When nothing is flying, the Hopi are just as wrong in using their words, as we are with one of ours. Of course, the more distinctions which are to be made, the more chance there is of mistake. The Eskimo may use the word for one kind of snow when another is present. Nevertheless he is talking of a world which is not relative to his conceptual system, and we too have access to it.

The fact that there are different conceptual systems does not of itself prove any kind of relativism. Conceptual relativists do not just affirm that some communities have concepts for which there may be no exact equivalent in another community. They also hold that each system creates its own criteria of truth and falsity. These findings of Whorf do not go to prove this; he might, however, argue that some of the Hopi categories indicate a more radical difference in thought. The Hopi language contains no reference to time. Instead of distinguishing between space and time, it puts into one category everything that is or has been accessible to the senses, and into another category what is in the future and *also* what we would call mental. The question is whether a world conceived of in such a way is too different from our own to allow any significant correlation. It is however misleading even to present the problem in these terms. The Hopi's *experience* of the world may be different. In the same way someone who thought that the everyday world was suffused with mystic forces might in some sense experience it differently from a hard-headed Western scientist. We may see the world differently from the Hopi, and count different things important, but the basic question is whether *what* we experience is different.

Unless the way a community (or an individual) views the world is considered a separate question from how the world is, the possibility of a mistake is ruled out. We could then never consider that the Eskimo *does* notice real differences between kinds of snow. Our world would have one kind of snow, and his many kinds. Questions about space and time are more complicated. If, however, our experience of the world and the world itself are not distinguished, we will necessarily become satisfied with our own conceptual system and its metaphysics, and others will be similarly self-satisfied. Alternative systems will be incomprehensible. No-one could ever judge their metaphysics to be in any way inadequate, since there would be no possible standard of judgment.

Once it is accepted that the world and experience of it, as expressed in a conceptual system, are distinct, it is clearly possible to correlate the different experience of individuals and of communities in the same circumstances. Although the way we severally describe the situation may be different, nevertheless we can accept that the situation is the same for everyone. Even if basic categories such as space and time are not distinguished by everyone, we can see what the rough equivalents are. Indeed, the whole of Whorf's account of the Hopi language assumes that it *is* possible to correlate different conceptual systems, and, as we have argued, this assumption presupposes the falsity of relativism. It does not matter how much it is stressed that it is very difficult to do this, or that we can only express in our language an approximation to their concepts. If the exercise is logically possible, relativism is false. Whorf's findings not only do not entail relativism, they depend on its falsity.

Once the notion of language applying to one public world is challenged, and limitations on what can be properly said are removed, language becomes impossible. It is for this reason that there is no point in arguing with the anti-rationalist. He cannot coherently state his case without already assuming that there is such a thing as truth, and that therefore good reasons for belief are possible. If he is right (and given his assumptions he could not be, since there would be no such thing as being 'right') his only course is silence.

Conclusion

If what I am committed to can be stated, my commitment must be subject to the presuppositions which make language possible. It will be based on beliefs which are objectively true or false and which are not merely valid for me and those who agree with me. Whether it is easy or difficult to establish the truth of a belief will clearly depend on its nature. The important point is that if it is a genuine belief, it is in principle within the scope of truth and falsity, it can be understood by those who do not hold it, and can therefore be rationally scrutinised. When someone is committed to Christianity, he shares the beliefs which themselves constitute Christianity, and if they are true, they are true for everyone, including atheists. If they are false, they are false even for Christians, even though they do not recognise it. If this were not so, there would be no clash between Christians and atheists, since they could not be disagreeing. Christianity is therefore not something very different from the way Christians conceive it. If it is saying anything at all, it must be making claims about what is objectively the case. Since the fact that these claims may be true also means that they could be false, Christianity is put at risk in a way which is uncongenial to some. At the same time as it is clear that since its claims are of far-reaching significance and could be true, they cannot be ignored by anyone concerned, as rationality demands, with what is true.

It is fashionable to fix one's attention on the fact of commitment. This is understandable. If our commitment determines what we regard as true, all that matters is whether a commitment is sincere, and it is perhaps significant that in some people's eyes sincerity is the only virtue, and hypocrisy the only vice. As we have seen, however, commitments involve claims to truth which are logically prior to the commitment. It follows that what ought to be of fundamental interest is whether the claims are true and the commitments justifiable.

Closely linked with questions about commitment are questions concerning concepts. Since we live in one world with which our beliefs may or may not correspond, the interesting question should not merely be what concepts we have, but also whether they properly reflect reality. In recent years the preoccupation of philosophers with conceptual analysis has sometimes blinded them to problems about the adequacy of our concepts. If there are different ways of conceiving reality, it is not enough to describe them. We cannot avoid choosing between them. To deny that this can be done on a rational basis involves us in the incoherence of conceptual relativism.

It can be dangerous to ignore the possibility that our concepts may be inadequate since it may result in our confusing questions about the existence and nature of concepts with questions about things themselves. Although it seems an obvious point to make, the concept of X is always distinct from X. Having a pain is different from having the concept of pain. Animals can presumably have pains without having the concept, while most of the time we have the concept but do not necessarily have a pain. It is possible, too, to have the concept of something which does not exist, such as a unicorn. We can even have the concept of nothing, and thinking of the concept of nothing is very different from thinking of nothing (or not thinking of anything). This kind of point is particularly important for the philosophy of religion. The fact that some men have a concept of God does not mean that He does exist, any more than the fact that no-one had a concept of God would mean that He did not exist. Confusion about this may be one of the reasons why in a sceptical age it has become fashionable to talk of 'the death of God'. Even if men have stopped thinking of God and the concept of God has 'died', it is nonsense to say that God has died. If an eternal being such as God ever existed, by definition He could not die. Whether He does exist is a separate issue from questions about the concepts men may or may not have.

What reality is like and how we conceive it are always separate questions. We ourselves cannot say what it is like independently of our conceptions of it. Our concepts provide as it were a window on the world which may well distort it. This does not mean that we cannot recognise the possibility that we are mistaken and we may even be able to discover our mistake for ourselves. Other concepts may prove more adequate, as when someone is converted to a religion or adopts a new scientific theory.

What in fact has been missing from so much recent controversy in religion, science and other fields, is the notion of objectivity – of things being the case whether people recognise them or not. This gives point to arguments which otherwise, if they were possible at all, would merely appear to result from clashes of different personalities or different social structures. Its role is more vital still, since it is indispensable for the existence of language. Without it there could be no criteria to distinguish knowledge from ignorance, and human reason becomes impotent. With it the claims of religion, the discoveries of science, the assumptions of moral argument, and much else, take on the importance they deserve.

Bibliography

Baier, K., *The Moral Point of View*, Ithaca, New York, 1958

Bartley, W. W., *The Retreat to Commitment*, New York, 1962; London, 1964

Beattie, J., *Other Cultures*, London, 1964

Beardsmore, R. W., *Moral Reasoning*, London, 1969

Braithwaite, R. B., 'An Empiricist's View of the Nature of Religious Belief', in *Christian Ethics and Contemporary Philosophy*, ed. I. T. Ramsey, London, 1966

Brown, S. C., *Do Religious Claims Make Sense?*, London, 1969

Feyerabend, P. K., 'Consolation for the Specialist', in *Criticism and the Growth of Knowledge*, ed. I. Lakatos and A. Musgrave, Cambridge, 1970

Flew, A. N. and MacIntyre, A., *New Essays in Philosophical Theology*, London, 1955

Hare, R. M., *The Language of Morals*, Oxford, 1952
'Theology and Falsification', in *New Essays in Philosophical Theology*, ed. A. N. Flew and A. MacIntyre, London, 1955
Freedom and Reason, Oxford, 1963

Hick, J. (ed.), *Faith and the Philosophers*, London, 1964

High, D. M., *Language, Persons and Belief*, New York, 1967

Kuhn, T. S., *The Structure of Scientific Revolutions*, Chicago, 1962
'Reflections on my Critics', in *Criticism and the Growth of Knowledge*, ed. I. Lakatos and A. Musgrave, Cambridge, 1970

Lakatos, I. and Musgrave, A. (eds.), *Criticism and the Growth of Knowledge*, Cambridge, 1970

Lévy-Bruhl, L., *Primitive Mentality* (trans. L. A. Clare), London, 1923

MacIntyre, A. (ed.), *Metaphysical Belief*, Ithaca, New York, 1959

Malcolm, N., 'Psychological Explanation of Religious Belief', in *Faith and the Philosophers*, ed. J. Hick, London, 1964

Martin, C. B., *Religious Belief*, Ithaca, New York, 1959

Mead, M., *Culture and Commitment*, London, 1970

Nowell-Smith, P., *Ethics*, Harmondsworth, London, 1954

Phillips, D. Z., *The Concept of Prayer*, London, 1965
(ed.), *Religion and Understanding*, Oxford 1967
Faith and Philosophical Enquiry, London, 1970
Death and Immortality, London, 1970

Phillips, D. Z. and Mounce, H. O., *Moral Practices*, London, 1969

Quine, W. V., *Word and Object*, Cambridge, Mass., 1960
Ontological Relativity, New York, 1969

Ramsey, I. T., *Religious Language*, London, 1957
(ed.), *Christian Ethics and Contemporary Philosophy*, London, 1966

Tillich, P., *The Dynamics of Faith*, London, 1957

Toulmin, S., *The Place of Reason in Ethics*, Cambridge, 1950

Trigg, R. H., *Pain and Emotion*, Oxford, 1970

Wilson, B. (ed.), *Rationality*, Oxford, 1970

Winch, P., *The Idea of a Social Science*, Oxford, 1958
'Understanding a Primitive Society', in *Religion and Understanding*, ed. D. Z. Phillips, Oxford, 1967

Wittgenstein, L., *Philosophical Investigations*, Oxford, 1958
Lectures and Conversations on Aesthetics, Psychology and Religious Belief, ed. C. Barrett, Oxford, 1966
On Certainty, Oxford, 1969

Whorf, B. L., *Language, Thought and Reality*, ed. J. Carroll, Cambridge, Mass., 1956

Index

agreement in judgements, 39, 64, 67

anarchistic theory of knowledge, 112

atheism, 50

Ayer, A. J., 146

Baier, K., 19

Bartley, W. W., 145–50

Beardmore, R. W., 19f., 22, 66–9, 71, 129f.

Beattie, J., 7–9, 13

'bliks', 93–4

Braithwaite, R. B., 32f., 36

Brown, S. C., 83f.

colour-words, 64

commitment, involving propositional belief, 43–6, 57–8, 97

concepts, conditions for learning, 19–21

conceptual relativism, 7, 12, 14–26

determinism, 138–45

disagreement, 66, 120ff., 135–6, 152–4; moral, 68–72, 128–31; religious, 125–7; scientific, 104ff.

faith, 54, 57

fanaticism, 62–3

Feyerabend, P., 109–14, 119, 161

Flew, A., 59

forms of life, 27, 40, 59, 64ff., 120

freedom, 112, 131–4, 137

'generation gap', 11–12

Grünbaum, A., 141f.

Hare, R. M., 61–3, 72, 93f., 121, 131–3

Heraclitus, 155f.

High, D. M., 65

Hughes, G. H., 33

hypocrisy, 75, 167

incommensurability, 100, 102, 109, 119, 161

intolerance, 135–7

justification of commitments, 53–63

Kuhn, T. S., 99–109, 113, 114–18, 119, 128, 131, 139, 140, 159f., 161

Lakatos, I., 106

language-games, 31, 59, 96

Last Judgment, 29

Levy-Bruhl, L., 8

Macintyre, A., 124–6, 133f.

Malcolm, N., 38f.

Martin, C. B., 85f.

Mead, M., 11f.

meaning, 50–3

moral concepts, 19

morality, 66–72

Morgan, D. N., 37

Mounce, H. O., 23f., 69

Nowell-Smith, P. H., 135f.

objectivism, 4, 15–18, 25, 135–7, 168

pain, concept of, 19

paradigms, 100, 103–6, 148

Paul, St, 79
Phillips, D. Z., 22–4, 35, 40f., 50, 52, 69, 73, 86–92, 101
Plato, 3, 155f.
progress, 116
Protagoras, 3, 23, 150, 155f.
psychology, 117, 123–4, 139–40

Quine, W. V., 157–9

Ramsey, I. T., 77–80
rationality, 113, 121, 142, 145–52
reality, 2, 9, 15
reasons, 58, 106–7, 121, 133, 137
red, concept of, 21
'reductionism', 32–6
relativism, 1–6, 22–6
religious belief, 27–32, 36–42
religious language, 72–81
Resurrection, 28, 36–7, 78–80, 125–7

scientific theories, 99ff.
social anthropology, 7–9, 13–14, 161

sociology, 139–40, 161
'solution', 130
subjectivism, 3, 6, 135, 150

Tillich, P., 56–8, 73
Toulmin, S., 65
translation, possibility of, 15, 157–66
truth, 15, 23, 86–96, 114–18, 126, 157–9

ultimate commitment, 43
ultimate concern, 56
unbeliever, 81–8

Whorf, B. L., 162–5
Winch, P., 15, 60, 66
Wittgenstein, L., 24, 27, 28–32, 35, 36f., 39f., 47–50, 53–5, 57–63, 64f., 72, 80, 88, 94–9, 119, 120, 122
world, one, 160ff.
worlds, different, 9, 14f., 86, 100, 152, 161, 163